Unlocking Opportunities for Growth

How to Profit from Uncertainty While Limiting Your Risk

Alexander B. van Putten and Ian C. MacMillan

Vice President, Publisher: Tim Moore
Associate Publisher and Director of Marketing: Amy Neidlinger
Wharton Editor: Yoram (Jerry) Wind
Executive Editor: Jim Boyd
Editorial Assistant: Myesha Graham
Operations Manager: Gina Kanouse
Digital Marketing Manager: Julie Phifer
Publicity Manager: Laura Czaja
Assistant Marketing Manager: Megan Colvin
Marketing Assistant: Brandon Smith
Cover Designer: Chuti Prasertsith
Managing Editor: Kristy Hart
Project Editors: Meg Shaw and Lori Lyons
Copy Editor: Keith Cline
Proofreader: San Dee Phillips
Indexer: Erika Millen
Senior Compositor: Gloria Schurick
Manufacturing Buyer: Dan Uhrig

© 2009 by Pearson Education, Inc.
Publishing as Wharton School Publishing
Upper Saddle River, New Jersey 07458

Wharton School Publishing offers excellent discounts on this book when ordered in quantity for bulk purchases or special sales. For more information, please contact U.S. Corporate and Government Sales, 1-800-382-3419, corpsales@pearsontechgroup.com. For sales outside the U.S., please contact International Sales at international@pearson.com.

Company and product names mentioned herein are the trademarks or registered trademarks of their respective owners.

Printed in the United States of America

First Printing July 2008

ISBN-10: 0-13-223790-3
ISBN-13: 978-0-13-223790-1

Pearson Education LTD.
Pearson Education Australia PTY, Limited.
Pearson Education Singapore, Pte. Ltd.
Pearson Education North Asia, Ltd.
Pearson Education Canada, Ltd.
Pearson Educatión de Mexico, S.A. de C.V.
Pearson Education—Japan
Pearson Education Malaysia, Pte. Ltd.

Library of Congress Cataloging-in-Publication Data

Putten, Alexander B. van.
  Opportunity engineering : how to profit from uncertainty without increasing risk / Alexander B. Van Putten And Ian C. Macmillan.
    p. cm.
  ISBN 0-13-223790-3 (hbk. : alk. paper) 1. Investment analysis. 2. Corporations—Valuation.
I. MacMillan, Ian C., 1940- II. Title.
  HG4529.P88 2009
  658.15'54—dc22
                          2008011016

To Lucinda, who makes all things possible.
—Alex van Putten

To Jean, who continues to put up with me—
I know not why.
—Ian MacMillan

Contents

Acknowledgments

There were many people who helped us with this book. The concept of Opportunity Engineering was made practical through the EVS software that was developed through the hard work and continuing dedication of Adrian Becker, a young man who understands both finance and software development, a rare breed in our experience. Adrian toiled for many months creating EVS that makes the valuation of opportunities both quick and intuitive. Alan Abrahams, at the time a visiting professor at Wharton and now at Virginia Tech, spotted Adrian's genius and mentored his efforts. Without the insight of interested industry practitioners, we would not have been able to develop the Opportunity Engineering methodology into a useful tool. In particular Paul Huck, the CFO, and Ron Pierantozzi, at the time Director of Business Development, at Air Products and Chemicals, Inc., were instrumental in developing our concepts. Paul Snaith and his team at Shell Global Solutions were very helpful in pointing out needed modifications to the EVS software that make it more useful.

We, of course, need to thank our editor Lynn Selhat who spent a great deal of time working with the original manuscript to arrive at the book in its present form. Many of the illustrations are the work of Laurie Wigham in San Francisco who has a talent for making business concepts look clear and attractive. Last but not least, Jerry Wind at Wharton School Publishing encouraged us to write this book to bring our work to a larger audience. In the same vein, we thank Jim Boyd, the executive editor at Pearson Education, who held his tongue as we encountered delays.

About the Authors

Alexander B. van Putten is an adjunct faculty member at the Wharton School of the University of Pennsylvania where he has been teaching graduate students since 1993. He is actively involved with Wharton's executive education programs where he lectures on issues surrounding innovation, corporate entrepreneurship, and strategic growth. He is a partner of Cameron & Associates LLC, which consults on strategy and business planning for clients ranging from Air Products & Chemicals, Shell Global Solutions to Seagate Technology, Novell, and Westcon. Prior to teaching at Wharton, van Putten was a general partner in equity and fixed income arbitrage and commercial mortgage securitization partnerships. He was also an SVP responsible for investments at Chrysler Capital Realty. Early in his career, he worked in the investment departments of Bankers Trust and Safeco Insurance Companies as well. van Putten has a BA in economics from Boston University, a MBA from the Wharton School, and is a DBA candidate at Edinburgh Business School. He has published articles in *Harvard Business Review* and *Research-Technology Management*.

Ian C. MacMillan is the academic director of the Sol C. Snider Entrepreneurial Research Programs at the Wharton School, University of Pennsylvania. He is also the Dhirubhai Ambani Professor of Innovation and Entrepreneurship in the Management Department. Formerly he was director of the Entrepreneurship center at NYU and taught at Columbia and Northwestern Universities and the University of South Africa. In 1999 he was awarded the Swedish Foundation for Small Business Research prize for his contribution to research in the area of entrepreneurship. Prior to joining the academic world, MacMillan was a chemical engineer and gained experience in gold and uranium mines, chemical and explosives factories, oil refineries, soap and food manufacturers, and the South African Atomic Energy Board. He has been a director of several companies in the travel, import/export, and pharmaceutical industries and has extensive consulting experience, having worked with such companies as DuPont, General Electric, GTE, IBM, Citibank, Metropolitan Life, Chubb & Son, American Re-Insurance, Texas Instruments, KPMG, Hewlett Packard, Intel, Fluor Daniel, Matsushita (Japan), Olympus (Japan), and L.G. Group (Korea). MacMillan's articles have appeared in the *Harvard Business Review, The Sloan Management Review, The Journal of Business Venturing, Administrative Science Quarterly, Academy of Management Journal, Academy of Management Review, Academy of Management Executive, Management Science and Strategic Management Journal*, among others. His most recent book, *Discovery-Driven Strategy*, is published by Harvard Business School Press, and can be considered the sister book to this one.

Foreword

The book you are holding is deliberately as short as we could make it because we assume our readers are busy and do not have much time to read. Instead of a longwinded discourse, you want results and to grow the top line. Despite its brevity, we hope we get the point across that you can engineer the financial returns of business investments much as you can engineer a product. Using the concepts of Opportunity Engineering (OE), you no longer need to accept the outcome of investments in R&D, M&A, new markets, new products, and strategic plans, as being largely the hand you are dealt. Instead, OE allows you to stack the deck in your favor, by limiting the downside while letting the upside run. The OE methodology is simple to use, yet disciplined, which makes it an effective management tool. This book is intended for both general and financial managers. General managers will find in it new ways of planning and directing business investments that creates maximum returns with reduced risk. The result will be a more agile organization that embraces change through true innovation. The OE concepts are as much, if not more, about a mindset and a culture than numbers. The financial manager will find a new way to look at uncertain investments through the updated valuation techniques found in OE that foster more effective management. We welcome your comments, questions, and suggestions, so feel free to get in touch: alexvp@wharton.upenn.edu.

1

Breaking the Go/No Go Vise Grip on Innovative Growth

This book is about extracting growing profits, sometimes big profits, from uncertainty while only marginally increasing business risk—by what we call *Opportunity Engineering*®.

A day does not go by without someone in the business media waxing eloquent about the pace of change, the increasing turbulence of technology, or the massive pressures of global competition. Writers and broadcasters go on and on about the increasing uncertainty this brings about, and all this uncertainty is generally couched as threatening. This foreshadowing is astonishing when you consider that boundless opportunities for big-win investments can lurk within uncertainty—uncertain yes, but with huge upside potential nonetheless.

We asked ourselves what causes firms and managers to generally regard uncertainty as a negative, when in fact opportunities for unusual prosperity lie in being able to exploit that very uncertainty. As we looked into the reasons why managers do not forge prosperity out of uncertain investments, we decided that it is really not their fault! We found that managers have not been given the right tools for investing in uncertain times. They are in the grips of a "Go/No Go vise," using tools for investment analysis that were created for more stable times. Discounted cash flow (DCF) calculations and net present value (NPV) analysis have them fixated on "making their numbers" or being treated as failures. These blinkers keep them locked into a Go/No Go decision-making pattern, either proceeding full steam ahead or stopping in their tracks (which, in the face of uncertainty, is usually *No Go*), when in fact they could be engineering the risk out of uncertain opportunities and going for high potential wins by slicing out their downside and boosting their upside.

The problem with the traditional approach (i.e., NPV) is that after an idea for a new product or service has been assessed and given the green light by senior management, and the development team lays out a project plan, they are expected to turn the idea into an asset that delivers expected returns; otherwise, they have failed. Figure 1.1 is an example of this classic Go/No Go thinking. It seems logical, but it has the unintended consequence of stopping innovation dead in its tracks, and it often piles up large losses, too. Why? Because if an idea has to turn into an asset "or else," the logical response is to focus on low-risk ideas that are close to a company's current offerings—those that are a safer bet. This conservatism might make sense for the individual manager, but if it becomes the norm it keeps companies focused on what worked in the past rather than focused on the future, where the opportunities for high growth lie. This risk avoidance snuffs out the experimentation and innovation that lay at the heart of all great companies' history, when their entrepreneurial spirit ran high. Indeed, from our consulting work, we suspect that many managers self-select out high-potential, uncertain ideas because they are afraid of being wrong and being criticized for it. This fear causes a narrow focus on incremental changes to existing products. The question is, can anything be done to change this deadly dynamic?

Figure 1.1   Go/No Go

Something can be done. For the past four years, we have been working on bringing you the right tool to manage beyond Go/No Go. We found it in something that we call Opportunity Engineering (OE), which allows you to assess uncertain opportunities and find ways of selecting only those where you can engineer the chance to capture their high upside potential *and* slice out the downside. OE allows you to select and pursue ideas that reach a long way into the upside potential and wrench out profits, while at the same time allow you to contain your risk to little more than your existing business risk.

Making Uncertainty Work for You

The key concept of OE is making uncertainty work *for* you rather than *against* you. In most uncertain projects, the potential profits have a probability distribution, as shown in Figure 1.2.

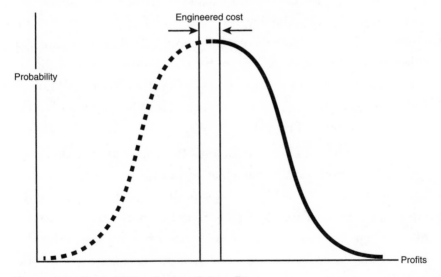

Figure 1.2   Probability of potential profits

If (and only if) you can Opportunity Engineer the project, you can in fact "slice out" the downside risk by engineering the opportunity so that the left tail of the distribution is removed, giving you an asymmetric return in which the actual probability of profits is confined to the opportunity space under the solid line of Figure 1.2. This opportunity space is bought at the engineered cost, which is all you need to risk to "buy" the rights to the potential upside offered by the project. If you cannot create this asymmetry, and the downside risk remains, you do *not* have an Engineered Opportunity, you have a WAG (wild-ass gamble)!

The importance of this insight is that now the more uncertain a project is, the better! Uncertainty widens the curve because there exists a larger universe of possible returns. More of the profits will be to the right along the curve where there is a greater chance of a higher profit, while there is no chance of a loss beyond the engineered cost. This probability distribution usually causes a good deal of discussion with executives we advise—it is a completely different way of thinking, but it makes sense as long as you can control the downside.

The same reasoning lies behind stock options in the financial markets: The greater the uncertainty surrounding a stock, the greater the option value, because the downside risk is limited to the price of the option.[1] Therefore, higher uncertainty allows for a bigger potential upside win with a controlled exposure to a downside loss, namely the option's cost. For the same price, would you rather have an option on Google (a proxy for high uncertainty) or on P&G (a proxy for low uncertainty)? Google, of course!

The disconnect between traditional financial valuations and management intuition results from a bias against uncertainty. But a situation that is uncertain *has* to have some positive context, or else it is not uncertain, it is just plain bad. Right? So as long as the risk reward profile is designed to have a limited downside exposure coupled with a high upside—the asymmetric return that we discussed earlier—the more uncertain the project, the better! We call this *positive uncertainty*. It is at the heart of the transformational effect of OE.

---

[1] Opportunity Engineering draws off the principles of real options analysis (ROA), which is a method for valuing uncertain investments, but goes well beyond valuation to deliberately reconstruct investments to increase their value and contain risk.

OE creates a safe harbor where high-payoff, innovative investments can be aggressively pursued, because it changes the development process.

Instead of considering just whether Go or No Go, a project could be broken down into stages and dropped cheaply if the early stages aren't working out, or a project once underway could be redirected to a different product or market, or the venture or the venture's intellectual property could be sold off, or the project could be scaled up or slowed down or postponed, or the project could spawn a joint venture or precipitate a merger with another company. Clearly, OE opens up many possibilities, and usually none of these possibilities are evaluated when Go/No Go thinking is the norm.

Go/No Go as a decision-making model is simply too constraining, but it's very understandable why companies stick with Go/No Go thinking. First of all, it's what we were all taught in finance and accounting courses. Second, it is relatively easy to manage, whereas managing uncertainty is not. The trick is to engineer into the project early indicators that convert the uncertainty into more certain knowledge, quickly and cheaply, so that you can redirect or shut down with minimum loss. In other words, fail fast, fail cheap, and move on to the real winners. That, in essence, is the key to OE and to this book.

Managing Uncertainty

OE is both a tactical approach and a mindset. In other words, it offers a specific way of valuing opportunities—we developed our own proprietary software that enables you to plug in the parameters of a project and determine its potential quickly and with minimal effort. Along the way, it helps inculcate a culture of innovation, where decision makers are not afraid to go after high-risk, high-opportunity bets.

In the next chapter, we show you how to begin this process of OE, but first let's take a look at why NPV and DCF are right for some situations but wrong for others.

NPV and DCF: When and When Not to Use Them

As we alluded to earlier, the overuse of discounted cash flow analysis that leads to the ubiquitous NPV calculation is simply inappropriate when applied to uncertain investments, whether they are new products, entering new markets, or launching bold strategies. We think these tools have done much to stifle the entrepreneurial spirit in many companies. This is a strong statement, and we get pushback from many financial managers because NPV is the metric used across the board, so why rock the boat? Of course, our response is that rocking the boat is exactly how to find opportunities, especially if you are the first to do so.

This is not to say that NPV should be abandoned—far from it. Ultimately, the uncertainty in innovative projects will be engineered down to a point where using NPV is perfectly appropriate!

When to use NPV: So, let's look at where DCF works and should be used. Discounted cash flow was "invented" to value corporate bonds. Here it is brilliant, because we know everything with a great deal of certainty. With a corporate bond, we know for sure what the time frame of the cash flow is by just looking at the indenture. If it is a 20-year bond, we have 240 monthly cash flow payments. The amount of each cash flow payment is also known for sure (from the indenture, by looking at the coupon rate). Therefore, the only unknown is the appropriate discount rate with which to present value the cash flows. Even this is easily determined in most cases by consulting one of the rating agencies such as Standard & Poor's that gives a risk rating to a bond (e.g., AA). With the rating in hand, we look in the newspaper and might see that the spread for AA corporate bonds is 1.50% over Treasuries. We then add that 1.50% spread to the corresponding risk-free maturity to get the appropriate discount rate for the bond. Simple.

This logic was really quite brilliant at the time, and it was soon extended to valuing other, riskier investments. For example, in the 1950s, if Goodyear was considering building a factory, it could be valued in much the same way as a bond. The number of tires that the factory could produce during its useful life could be determined in advance from the plant capacity, and the profit margin from each tire could also be known with some assurance during those relatively stable times. With that information, it would be possible to model the cash flows to be derived from the factory during its life: [(Number of tires per year) x (Useful life of the factory) x (Expected margin per tire)]. The appropriate discount rate to adjust for risk could be determined from the rating given to Goodyear at the time to arrive at the correct spread over the corresponding Treasury rate. With the cash flows and the discount rate in hand, it was possible to arrive at the present value of the factory, which if greater than the cost of the factory provided a positive NPV to the company, leading to the conclusion that the factory should be built. This all makes complete sense and is entirely appropriate in low-uncertainty environments.

When NPV does not work: DCF completely unravels when uncertainty rises and the original logic behind using NPV as a valuation methodology falls apart. As uncertainty increases, it becomes impossible to forecast future cash flows and their timing with any degree of confidence. In addition, high uncertainty makes it all but impossible to arrive at the appropriate discount rate. Worse still, the theory behind DCF analysis calls for the discount rate to increase along with uncertainty to adjust for the risk in the investment. The result is that uncertain investments are penalized with very high discount rates that diminish their perceived value. As a result, many interesting opportunities go unexplored because of what could be called "false negatives."

Furthermore, the NPV formula reflects only one view of the future. In practice, managers may plug "high," "most likely," and "low" cash flow estimates into the formula to come up with three NPV values. Although this is better than taking one look into the future, it still presumes one unalterable course of action; we start the project and finish the project, which has three different outcomes (high, most likely, and low), and we cannot change direction along the way. NPV cannot effectively account for the value of being able to alter course during the investment implementation effort. There is no way to capture the value of flexibility that would allow for redirection, abandonment, speeding up, slowing down, and so on. Our solution starts by applying OE to harness the upside potential in your business.

In the next chapter, you learn about the underlying principles of OE. Before that, however, we want to stress that OE is not by any means some wild-eyed new theory. It draws off a lot of very solid work done over the years by many scholars who have used approaches such as decision trees, decision and risk analysis (DRA), real options analysis, and scenario analysis. OE's main contribution is to extend beyond these approaches in two ways:

1. OE does not passively "accept" the parameters of the problem and proceed to valuing the opportunity, but rather challenges you to use the tools and your imagination to reengineer the opportunity and increase its value while driving down the risk. This is particularly valuable as a follow-on to scenario analysis.

2. The valuation of the opportunity, using the methodology we recommend, allows you to massively reduce the calculative complexity usually associated with DRA and real options approaches.

As this book unfolds, it will become apparent that the OE mindset has applications to almost all areas of business when uncertainty surrounds the outcome of the investment. In particular, OE will be of great value when selecting and managing R&D projects, mergers and acquisitions, and joint ventures and alliances. OE will also prove its value when entering new markets; designing, monitoring, and guiding major contract negotiations; and with strategic planning and scenario planning. How OE impacts these sorts of investments is discussed in detail in Chapter 6, "Applying Opportunity Engineering Throughout Your Business."

2

The Opportunity Engineering Process

In our executive education classes at Wharton, we use the following simplified case to illustrate what we mean by Opportunity Engineering (OE). The example is based on a real situation but is vastly simplified. We could easily make the argument a lot more complex, at great cost to understandability, but we want it to be simple to follow.

Illustrative Case Study 1: Entering a Foreign Market

An Innovation team thinks that they can enter the Chinese market with a new cement additive product that they have developed.

There is a 5% chance that the adoption rate in this new market will be rapid. The expected Net Present Value (NPV) for this product is $1,400 if the adoption is in fact rapid and they can cash in before imitators compete away the profits. If it is slow, imitators will move in fast while adoption is grinding along, and the NPV will be for all intents and purposes zero.

An additive plant can be quickly assembled in a matter of weeks. The cost to assemble an additive plant is $200. Should we go for the Chinese market?

Our question is this: How would you look at this opportunity? The prevailing view relies on conventional NPV thinking that we see reflected in Equation 1.

Equation 1

$$NPV = \text{Expected discounted cash flow (DCF) of net revenues}$$
$$- \text{Total DCF cost}$$
$$= (0.05 \times \$1400) - \$200$$
$$= \$70 - \$200$$
$$= -\$130$$

In any NPV-driven company, this opportunity would be dead on arrival. However, the issue was that management intuitively thought that this was a good opportunity for the company. How do we reconcile the calculated NPV against the intuition of seasoned managers? What if we instead begin to engineer the opportunity to separate some of the risk from the reward?

Suppose, like many firms might, we decide to do a quick market test by shipping a batch of the product and test marketing it in one of the smaller Chinese cities to check the rate of adoption. This will cost $40. So, we are suggesting that we could explore the potential of this market entry without risking the full $200, by doing a bit of Opportunity Engineering and thus designing away some of the risk.

OE thinking changes the way in which the investment is developed, in this case by "spending a little to learn a lot" about the market. OE thinking suggests that the decision to invest be broken down into several different stages, rather than be considered as one larger Go/No Go decision. Here, the first stage is to invest $40 to test market the product and then evaluate the results before deciding to invest $200 in the plant. If we do this, the valuation changes markedly to what we call the *Engineered Value*®, as shown Equation 2.

Equation 2

$$\text{Engineered Value (EV)} = -\$40 + 0.05 (-\$200 + \$1400)$$
$$= -\$40 + \$60$$
$$= \$20$$

Now we first risk $40 to explore the new market, which is lost if we decide not go forward. But we will not be investing the $200 unless we are confident that the market will rapidly adopt our additive and we can cash in before imitators compete away our profits. True, the team is giving this only a 5% probability of occurring, but then we have only a 5% chance of investing the $200, right? As a result, our payoff changes markedly because we have a 5% chance of investing $200 *and* we have a 5% chance of earning $1,400. As we see it, the resulting payoff now becomes $20, much better than the *negative* $130 we had before. We have in effect used the $40 to engineer a call on the plant construction. Like a financial call, this "engineered call" gives us the right but not the obligation to invest further if, and only if, the results are positive for us.

With this, we create Opportunity Value because it exists only if things go well with the market test. At the same time, we have adjusted the NPV to reflect the 5% chance of incurring the cost to assemble the plant, so we call this Net Present Value engineered (NPVe). Now we can define EV in the following way:

Engineered Value = NPVe + Opportunity Value

What if we further engineer this opportunity to design out even more risk? By this, we mean how can we reduce the risk in the investment while retaining the same reward? The problem with this new market is the high risk of getting rapidly imitated, and that is reflected in the short 5% odds of success. Suppose the team comes to you and suggests that even if we get imitated fast, they have identified a Chinese subsidiary of a multinational that is interested in licensing the product regardless of whether it has been rapidly imitated; and because they will be obliged to honor our intellectual property (IP), they cannot imitate us. The team admits that nothing is certain, but they believe there is a 50/50 chance that the multinational will license the product, allowing us to extract an NPV of $60 in licensing fees. What our clever development team has done is mitigate the downside risk of being rapidly imitated. We consider this to be creating Abandonment Value (AV); it's a way of extracting value from the project by recovering some of the investment if we choose not to go forward.

We can now expand our definition of EV to include the Abandonment Value, so our equation becomes

Engineered Value = NPVe + Opportunity Value + Abandonment Value

Figure 2.1 shows how the OE process changes the dynamics of the project.

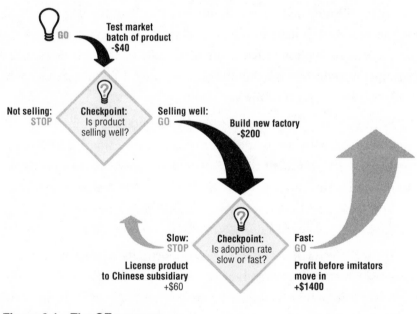

Figure 2.1   The OE process

As shown in Equation 3, it substantially expands the Engineered Value of this new market entry.

Equation 3

$$EV = -\$40 + 0.05\,(-\$200 + \$1400) + 0.95 \times (0.5 \times \$60)$$
$$= -\$40 + \$60 + \$28.50$$
$$= \$48.50$$

Now the test market looks a great deal more appealing. Let's see how we brought about this change. The first $40 is still at risk no matter what happens, same as before, and we still have only a 5% chance of both spending the remaining $200 to build the plant and gaining the NPV of $1,400 if we succeed. However, let's consider the last term, which calculates the AV resulting from the possibility of licensing the product if we do get rapidly imitated. If there is a 5% chance that we will *not* get rapidly imitated, i.e., 0.05(–$200 + $1400), there has to be a 95% chance that we *will* get rapidly imitated; however, because there is only a 50% chance that the Chinese subsidiary will actually go through with a license, we have to reflect that in the third term, too, so it becomes 0.95 x (0.5 x $60) = $28.50, reflecting the 95% chance of getting rapidly imitated and the 50% chance that the multinational will carry through with a license. This is what OE is about—looking for creative ways to reduce risk.

Encouraged, the team pushed OE even further—they met with the multinational interested in licensing the product and proposed a deal: If we pay them an up-front signing fee of $15, the subsidiary will guarantee to license the Chinese rights for $60 should we elect not to undertake production. Now we have guaranteed a way out; the subsidiary has guaranteed to license the product rights, but we are not required to license them. In the financial markets, this is called a put option, and we borrow that term here, calling it an *engineered put*. Let's see what this does to the value of the project (see Equation 4).

Equation 4

$$EV = (-\$40 - \$15) + 0.05 \times (-\$200 + \$1400) + 0.95 \times (\$60)$$
$$= -55 + \$60 + \$57 = \$62$$

Adding the engineered put option to the project has stepped up the value substantially to $62. The big change is in the third term, which is now 0.95 x (60). Because of the $15 payment to the Chinese subsidiary, we can now drop the 50% chance that they will not license the product when the time comes. The third term is now simply (0.95 x $60), and it is the converse of the 5% odds that the test market will succeed.

From this example, you see the principles behind OE and the dramatic increase in value that it can create if it takes hold in your company. It is a mindset as much as it is a financial and management tool; one that allows you to avoid many of those Go/No Go decisions that lead to the huge wastage and manifold foregone opportunities reported by the Product Development and Management Association, that many companies spend *half* of their development capital on failed product development, whereas best-of-breed innovators spend only about 20% of their resources on losing efforts.[1]

OE challenges managers at all levels of a company to ask how the downside can be mitigated or the upside increased. As our super-simplified example illustrated, the cost is usually worth it. Now let's consider a more complex case.

Illustrative Case Study 2: New Production Process

Let's look at an example of how a large industrial company used OE to engineer a project that was destined for the reject bin. After several years of R&D, the company thought that it had developed a new and promising method of converting a nasty by-product from refineries into clean energy. The substance is toxic, it tends to pile up around refineries, and it cannot be readily stored onsite for indefinite periods because it has the tendency to leach into ground water and pollute surface-water runoff from the site.

[1] Yasmin Gharehmani, "What's the Big Idea?" CFO, July 2006.

The R&D team began the project with the premise that any company that could find a use for the material would be rewarded with a commercial success, in part because of the zero or negative cost of goods sold. The lab had developed the technology and the IP needed to convert the substance into a clean fuel source to generate electricity, and they were confident that the technology would scale up to be of use in commercial applications. The company had already spent $3 million on the R&D to get the project to the point where the IP could be patented, so tangible value had been created.

However, a major issue prevented senior management from giving approval to spend another $3 million to build a pilot plant. The pilot plant would demonstrate commercial viability by validating scalability of the technology, and the lab was confident that the pilot plant would work as intended. The issue facing management was not the cost of the pilot plant but the cost of obtaining state and federal Environmental Protection Agency (EPA) permits needed before construction could begin on new power plants that would use this technology to convert this type of petroleum waste into a clean fuel source to generate electricity. A variety of sources estimated the cost of getting permits to be in the range of $60 million and could take three to four years of determined effort. What made the investment in the permitting processing even more daunting was the knowledge that no new power plants had been granted permits in several years, and the permitting process was therefore highly open-ended and difficult to define. Given these factors, the odds of successfully acquiring the needed permits to operate could not be determined.

With this background, management was leaning toward a decision to end further investment in the technology and just writing off the $3 million spent on R&D to date. In counterpoint to this decision was the project team's strong belief in the future of the technology, due to its ability to convert toxic petroleum wastes of many types into clean energy. Their contention was that the pilot plant should be built to demonstrate commercial viability; at which time, if successful, investment partners could be found who would participate in the cost of the permitting process, thereby sharing the risk in exchange for an equity position. The project team had already identified an investment bank that had expressed interest in making an investment in the project provided feasibility could be demonstrated through a successful pilot plant.

The way to break the logjam was to use OE to demonstrate the value of a successful pilot plant, which would establish technical viability in and of itself. We suggested that if the pilot plant were successful, it would have AV regardless of the decision to invest in the permitting process (for instance, finding alternative uses for the technology, should the company decide not to further invest in the project). If the company chose not to go ahead with the full investment in the permitting process, when the pilot plant was completed they could in essence then sell the IP to another company at a predetermined price. This is a very plausible option: In the past, companies have been able to create AV by donating the IP related to discontinued R&D projects to universities as the foundation for further research. The donated IP formed the basis of a tax deduction that created value by lowering the company's tax bill. In this case, that idea was not possible, so we challenged the project team to identify alternative users of the technology where gaining the needed permits to operate the proposed power plant would be less onerous. Any alternative users needed to have abundant sources of this material available that required disposal, a demonstrable market for electric power, and a simpler and less-costly permitting process. The team quickly found that the technology would be an asset to the oil companies that were developing the tar sands of Alberta, Canada, as a source of petroleum. The large amount of by-products generated from the refining process was substantially the same. They also identified oil refineries in Mexico that generated substantial amounts of the material and had less-onerous permitting challenges. The identification of these large, plausible abandonment opportunities engineered the project to a contender for funding.

A note of caution is appropriate here: For abandonment value to be considered, we believe that the potential source of value needs to be documented and demonstrated as unequivocally as possible. Otherwise, a danger exists that AV will be fabricated from the project team's hopes and dreams.

In this case, the project team was able to gain hard documentation from several sources to corroborate the value of the technology to other companies if the pilot plant were successful. With that information, it was possible to estimate an AV at $5 million to yield a positive EV. The way in which we computed the AV is covered later in Chapter 7, "Project Valuation Using EVS Software," but the importance of the number at this point is that it gave senior management multiple paths to choose from. They could

1. Stop the project at this point, which would require the write-off of the $3 million invested to date. (Note that this write-off is *not* included in the valuation; you cannot burden future decisions with past investments).

   Or

2. Build the pilot plant for another $3 million to validate that the technology would work in a large-scale facility.

   If the pilot plant worked as intended, the company would have several more engineered opportunities for itself.

3a. Not invest in permitting, but create $5 million AV by selling the IP to an unequivocally identified purchaser.

3b. Invest $60 million in the permitting process and build power plants itself if it were approved.

   Or

3c. Invest $60 million in the permitting process, and if not approved create $5 million AV by selling the IP to an unequivocally identified purchaser.

   Or

3d. Create an engineered call by looking for partners to help shoulder the cost of the permitting process in exchange for an equity ownership in the power plants.

3e. There was also a small chance that the pilot plant would not work as intended, in which case the company would lose an additional $3 million.

Note that neither the option to abandon nor the option to find an equity partner in the permitting process could be created if the pilot plant were not constructed.

Now management's decision was simplified between a certain $3 million write-off if the project were stopped at this point and, at worst, a $1 million loss if the pilot plant were built and it worked as expected and the technology was then sold (abandoned) to another company at that point. Further fueling a positive decision was the possibility that an equity partner would be engaged after the pilot plant was built that would invest the money to obtain the required permits but enable the company to retain an equity interest in the deal. Given these choices, management elected to build the pilot plant.

Another Source of Engineered Value: Trade or Sale of Uncertain Assets for Cash or Equity in Other Assets

Engineered Value can also be created when managers find a way for an uncertain asset to be traded for cash or equity in another company. GlaxoSmithKline, for example, developed an experimental antibiotic that showed promise in treating drug-resistant staphylococcal infections but was thought unlikely to become the sort of blockbuster drug the company needed to support its own growth rate. Rather than consign the IP to its library of interesting but unwanted compounds, it generated AV by trading the patents, technology, and marketing rights to develop this antibiotic for equity in Affinium, a privately held biotech company.[2] In this case, Glaxo very cleverly engineered the project return profile to avoid a loss and create a gain.

IBM is another firm that has aggressively recognized AV and is now generating more than $1 billion per year from its program to sell off unwanted IP, while other firms sit on mountains of potential AV.

The management issue you face is how to instill OE into your company's culture without losing control. We deal with that in Chapter 5, "Creating an Engineered Growth Portfolio." First, we need to look at how to carry out OE.

OE for an uncertain investment comprises two major steps: discovery-driven planning (DDP) and CheckPointing:

- **Stage 1:**   The DDP stage is devoted to developing the framework that defines the scope of the investment opportunity, develops the key drivers of potential profits, documents the key assumptions being made, and teases out the key challenges and major vulnerabilities of the project. In many cases, the DDP shows that the project does not qualify for further attention and should be set aside so that you can pursue more attractive opportunities. However, if the project looks promising, the next stage is CheckPointing.

- **Stage 2:**   The CheckPointing stage is where you begin to apply OE to structure ways of ramping up your reach into the upside potential while eradicating your downside risk. The way this is done is to carry out the two processes in parallel: First, systematically structure engineered calls, engineered puts, and engineered abandonments that add value and increase the reach into the potential of the project. Second, identify key CheckPoints where the major assumptions you developed in the DDP

---

[2]   Scott Hensley, "Glaxo Swaps Antibiotic Project for Equity Stake in Affinium," *Wall Street Journal*, February 26, 2003.

are going to be tested, so as to reduce uncertainty ahead of major resource commitments, thus reducing the risk of a costly failure. In Chapter 3, "How to Engineer Opportunities, Stage 1: DDP" we look at how to do DDP, and in Chapter 4, "How to Engineer Opportunities, Stage 2: CheckPointing," we look at CheckPointing.

3

How to Engineer Opportunities, Stage 1: DDP

Framing Your Challenges and Your Key Vulnerabilities

In this chapter, we start learning how to develop a Discovery-Driven Plan (DDP), which forms the platform of the Opportunity Engineering (OE) process. In the next chapter, we look at the Check-Pointing process, which is stage two of the process.

The DDP stage of OE comprises two substages:

1. **Framing and Operating Specification stage**, which scopes out the investment and documents your major assumptions

2. **Sensitivity Analysis stage**, which identifies the most critical assumptions you have made

Again, we will present a real case, which we deliberately simplified for purposes of understandability.

Ergonomic Desk Project

Coppice Consolidated (Coppice) is a furniture manufacturer looking to expand from its current household line (made from wood)

to office furniture, and has worked with a highly respected design and engineering firm to come up with a designer desk (made from molded polymer) for highly desktop computer-intensive workplaces.

They have little knowledge of the office furniture business, or of the molding production process, but they have an opportunity to license a unique design that will allow them to offer a more ergonomic desk, which in particular will appeal to high-paid professionals like architects, software and other engineers, and media artists and designers. They also think they can market it at a lower cost than the most competitive existing offerings because the licensor has developed a numerically controlled manufacturing system that will allow them to produce this higher-quality desk with fewer manufacturing workers than existing production systems.

Framing the Project

The firm currently generates $50 million in profits and has decided that any projects that take them down unknown and uncertain paths should at least have prospects of delivering a minimum 10% increment in profits (i.e., $5 million) by the fifth year of operation. Otherwise, why bother, when you could just reinvest in the existing business? Because they are currently making 15% return on assets (ROA) and 20% return on sales (ROS), management is basically not interested in uncertain new efforts that will not deliver at least 33% ROA and 20% ROS.

A DDP starts with this framing premise—namely, it starts by specifying required profits and profitability and works back to necessary revenues and allowable costs and assets. Thus, Table 3.1 depicts the performance challenges that the Office Desk project must meet to be worth the risk and effort. Note that we have flagged the columns in the top row of the figure with column letters *A* through *F*. These flags indicate what appears in this and all following columns in this chapter:

Column A flags the row number in the plan.

Column B provides the explanatory text for the number in Column C.

Column C contains the relevant numbers for the plan.

Column D identifies and flags every single assumption being made, and which needs to be tested as the plan unfolds.

Column E shows any benchmark data used to derive the number in Column C.

Column F either shows the source of the benchmark data appearing in column E, or it shows how the number in Column C was calculated, using the row numbers in Column A.

As you can see in Table 3.1, the second discipline of DDP is to identify and flag every assumption you are making. The discipline is to begin engineering the plan so that you 1) have the lowest possible costs to test the assumptions before any major investment, 2) can redirect your plan as the true reality unfolds from the uncertainty from which you started, and 3) find ways to create engineered calls, puts, and abandonment value as the plan develops.

TABLE 3.1   Framing the Office Desk Business

Column A	Column B	Column C	Column D	Column E	Column F
			Assumption Number	Bench-mark	Source or Formula
F17	Required Operating Profits	$5,000,000	1		Policy Decision
F18	Required ROA	33.3%	2	20.0%	Policy Decision
F19	Required ROS	20.0%	3	15.0%	Policy Decision
F20	Allowable Assets	$15,015,015			F17/18
F21	Necessary Sales Revenues	$25,000,000			F17/19
F22	Allowable Costs	$20,000,000			F21–F17

As you can see, if we assume (assumptions 1, 2, 3) that management will hold firm on their framing parameters for profits and profitability increments, *by year 6* the Office Desk business will need to generate $25 million in revenues without incurring more than $20 million in costs or requiring more than $15 million in assets. Note again that this is the *required* performance by year 6. If any DDP looks like it will not be able to deliver the profit and profitability bogeys by about year 5 to 7, no further planning is necessary—drop the project and go on to something with more promise!

The time frame of five to seven years depends on the competitive pace in the industry you are entering. In extreme cases, it could be as little as two years (consumer electronics), in others much longer (mining), but it needs to reflect the time you think it will reasonably take for the revenues from the project to reach a steady state or steady growth. If it looks like the profit and profitability bogeys are doable, this justifies more detailed planning.

Mapping Out the Consumption Chain

After you have framed the challenge, the next step is to map out the proposed *Consumption Chain* of your major market segments. The Consumption Chain maps out the entire set of experiences with your offering and your company that each major market segment undergoes, and it may differ from segment to segment. We discuss the Consumption Chain in more detail in the appendix at the end of this chapter.

The innovation will never be a fully commercialized business until every link in this Consumption Chain, from awareness of the need for the offering to final disposal of any used-up vestige, has been completed. Unless you or some agent delivers every link, the Consumption Chain is broken and therefore useless. But, each link incurs a cost to you or your agent. Each commercialized offering has its own particular link and differs markedly depending on whether it is a physical product, a physical or financial service, an interactive Web offering, a software package, and so on. What is important is to map the chain for your offering and ensure that you have plans to deliver it. For the Office Desk project, the Consumption Chain is mapped out in Figure 3.1.

Consumption Chain

Figure 3.1   Consumption Chain for Office Desk project

The Consumption Chain mapping provides the basis for building what we call the operations specification, the part of the DDP spreadsheet that specifies the physical activities that must take place for the Consumption Chain to actually be delivered to the market. In the Office Desk case, inspection of the proposed chain suggested that the following activities would be needed and be included in the spreadsheet (see Figure 3.2):

Advertising to create awareness and provoke search
Sales force to provoke selection and order/purchase
Delivery to enable delivery, receipt and installation
Manufacturing to create desks for customer use
Administration to handle complaints, returns, replacements

There would be no need for disposal because customers would handle their own disposal.

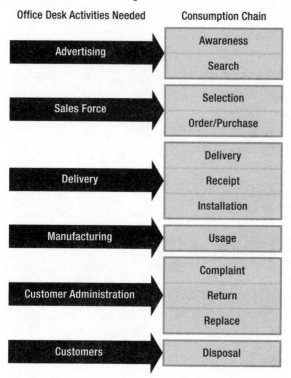

Figure 3.2   Consumption Chain for Office Desk project

Develop an Operations Specification

The operations specification starts with a calculation of the scope of what is required to make the bogeys and systematically works down the Consumption Chain, making best guess assumptions on the physical activities required and their associated costs.[1] Table 3.2 shows the evolution of the marketing and sales links of the operations specification.

---

[1]   The process is discussed in detail in the sister book to this, *MarketBusters*, by Rita Gunther McGrath and Ian C. MacMillan, Harvard Business School Press, 2005; and is also covered in reasonable depth in Chapter 10 of *The Entrepreneurial Mindset*, by McGrath and MacMillan, Harvard Business School Press, 2000; and in the *HBR* article "Discovery Driven Planning" by McGrath and MacMillan, *Harvard Business Review*, 1995.

TABLE 3.2   Scope Specification and Marketing Costs

	Operations Specifications			Assumption Number	Bench-mark	Source or Formula
F24	Wholesale Selling Price per Desk	$400		4	$420	Current Price
F25	Required Desk Sales	62,500	DESKS			F21/F24
F26	Desks Sold per Day (250-day year)	250				F25/F35
	Selling and Marketing Costs					
F29	Advertising as % of Sales	10.0%		5	6%	Industry Average
F30	Total Advertising	$2,500,000				F21°F29
F32	Desks per Order	2	DESKS	6	3	Distributors
F33	Sales Calls per Order	7	CALLS	7	5	Distributors
F34	Sales Calls per Day	4	CALLS	8	5	Distributors
F35	Sales Days per Year	250		9		
F36	Desks Sold per Salesperson/Year	286				[(F35°F34)/F33]°F32
F37	Sales Force Required	219				F25/F36
F38	Sales Commission	15.0%		10	10.0%	Competitors
F39	Salesperson Salary	$20,000		11	$20,000	Competitors
F40	Total Commissions	$3,750,000				F21°F38
F41	Total Salaries	$4,375,000				F37°F39
F42	Total Selling Costs	$8,125,000				F40+F41

The Office Desk team started with the assumption (row F24) that despite their superiority of product, as newcomers to the office desk business, they would still be buying their way into the market in year 6 by discounting off the competition and selling at $400 per desk (assumption 4). This means that to make their required revenue numbers, they would have to sell 62,500 desks per year or 250 per day.

Row F29 takes the desks per year challenge and begins to flesh out the assumed marketing activities needed. First, because office equipment manufacturers spend 6% of revenues on advertising, the Office Desk team assumed as low-share players they would have to be spending at least 10%.

Now comes an important part of DDP: *As someone with more expertise than the Office Desk team, you might disagree with assumptions 4 and 5.* In the spirit of DDP, voicing your objections is important. With *every* assumption, people are encouraged to voice their best estimate and the logic behind this estimate—and the resulting discussion thereby extracts the expertise of the team and its advisors. At the conclusion of the discussion, the team can then decide on their best estimate of the *range* of the assumption, because we are not confined to point estimates. This has three benefits:

1. The width of the range reflects the uncertainty of that assumption. These same range estimates will be the basis on which the project can be valued using our project evaluation software, Engineered Value Solver (EVS), which is discussed in detail in Chapter 7, "Project Valuation Using EVS Software," and available online (www.oppengine.com) to purchasers of this book. (As a reminder, you can use *any* evaluation software; however, ours is simple and user-friendly for handling complex, multibranch opportunities.)

2. When the DDP is completed, we can run a simulation of the plan and thereby get the sensitivity of our plan to the ranges of the assumptions.

3. Most important, we can design and insert CheckPoints into the plan, which allows us to test the most critical assumptions ahead of major investments. At each CheckPoint, we can engineer moves to create engineered calls, engineered puts, and engineered abandonment plays.

So, rows F32 through F42 show how the Office Desk team systematically went about making and flagging assumptions about the sales force structure: number of calls per sale, number of calls per day, order size, sales commissions and salaries; in many cases backed up by approximate industry data obtained from furniture distributors. Each of these assumptions can be challenged, and each should result in a range reflecting the team's uncertainty.

Table 3.3 shows how the rest of the income statement unfolded, estimating plant and manufacturing costs, delivery costs, and administrative costs. The masochists among you are welcome to go through the figure in detail, if you wish!

TABLE 3.3 Continuation of the Operations Specifications

Continuation of the Operations Specifications		Assumption Number	Bench-mark	Source or Formula
	Manufacturing costs	$105	12	$100	Suppliers
F46	Raw Materials per Desk	$10	13	$10	Suppliers
F47	Pallet Cost per Desk	$7,187,500			[+F46+F47]°F25
F48	Total Materials Costs				
F50	Desks per Day per Production Line	100	14	$80	Equipment supplies
F51	Production Days per Year	250	15	$250	Industry practice
F52	Number of Lines	3			F25/[F50°F51]
F53	Manufacturing Staff per Line	10	16	$20	
F54	Total Manufacturing Staff	25			F52°F53
F55	Manufacturing Salaries	$36,000	17	$25,000	Workers
F56	Manufacturing Salary Costs	$900,000			F54°F55
	Equipment Charges				
F60	Equipment Cost per Production Line	$2,500,000	18	$900,000	Equipment supplies
F61	Total Equipment	$6,250,000			F52°F60
F62	Depreciation Rate	10.0%	19	10.0%	Industry practice
F63	Annual Depreciation	$625,000			F61°F62

TABLE 3.3 Continuation of the Operations Specifications

Continuation of the Operations Specifications			Assumption Number	Bench-mark	Source or Formula
Delivery costs					
F67	Deliveries per Year	2142	ORDERS		F25/F32
F68	Delivery charges per Delivery	$80	20	$50	Delivery Firm
F69	Delivery Costs per Year	$171,360			F67°F68

Finally, Table 3.4 shows the calculations for the Income Statement that was derived from the preceding tables, and Table 3.5 shows equivalent assumptions and calculations for the balance sheet.

TABLE 3.4 Income Statement

	Income Statement		
F75	Revenues	$25,000,000	F17/F19
F76	Allowable Costs	$20,000,000	F21-F17
F77	Selling Costs	$8,125,000	F40+F41
F78	Advertising Costs	$2,500,000	F21°F29
F79	Materials Costs	$7,187,500	[+F46+F47]°F25
F80	Manufacturing Salaries	$900,000	F54°F55
F81	Delivery Costs	$171,360	F67°F68
F82	Depreciation Charges	$625,000	F61°F62
F83	Maximum Allowable Other Costs	$491,140	[F76–F77–F78–F79
	Profit	$5,491,140	–F80–F81–F82]
	ROS	22.0%	

TABLE 3.5 Balance Sheet Specifications

	Bottom Up Balance Sheet	Assumption	Assumption Number	Benchmark	Source or Formula
F89	Days Inventory	90	21	90	Bank
F90	Days Receivables	90	22	60	Bank
	Balance Sheet				
F90	Allowable Assets	$15,015,015			F17/F18
F92	Receivables	$6,250,000			(F75/360)°F90
F93	Inventory	$1,796,875			(F79/360)°F89
F94	Equipment	$6,250,000			F52°F60
F95	Allowable Other Assets	$718,140			[F90–F92–F93–F94]
	ROA	38%			

The spreadsheets reflected in the preceding tables yielded the following key outputs:

Projected profits	$5.9 million
Projected ROS	22%
Projected ROA	38%

So, the project just met the threshold returns, *which justified further planning effort.* If it did not, the team should either scrap the project and go on to something better or find creative ways to improve potential performance.

Document the Ranges for Each Assumption

As you progress through the DDP and document your assumptions, also document the ranges the team and their advisors agree on, yielding a list of assumptions with their most likely values and their highest and lowest values, like the Office Desk team did in Table 3.6.

TABLE 3.6   Assumption Ranges

Assumption Number	Assumption Ranges	Most Likely	Lowest	Highest
1	Required Operating Profits	$5,000,000	$4,500,000	$7,500,000
2	Required ROA	33%	30%	40%
3	Required ROS	0	0.18	0.25
4	Wholesale Selling Price per Desk	$400	$375	$450
5	Advertising as % of Sales	10%	8%	15%
6	Desks per Order	2	1	3
7	Sales Calls per Order	7	5	7
8	Sales Calls per Day	4	3	5
9	Selling Days per Year	250	250	250
10	Sales Commissions	15%	12%	18%
11	Sales Salary	$20,000	$20,000	$25,000
12	Raw Materials per Desk	$105	$80	$120
13	Pallet Cost per Desk	$10	$10	$12
14	Desks per Day per Production Line	100	100	120
15	Production Days per Year	250	250	250
16	Manufacturing Staff per Line	10	10	12
17	Manufacturing Salaries	$36,000	$32,000	$38,000
18	Equipment Cost per Production Line	$2,500,000	$2,000,000	$3,000,000
19	Depreciation Rate	10%	8%	12%
20	Delivery Charges per Order	$80	$50	$80
21	Days Inventory	90	60	90
22	Days Receivables	90	75	90

Sensitivity Analysis

The ranges from Table 3.6 can now be used to simulate the distribution of profits and profitability that stem from the assumptions. Any Monte Carlo package can be used. The output from such a Monte Carlo simulation is twofold:

1. The projected distribution of the outcomes in which you are interested (in the Office Desk case profits, ROA and ROS)

2. A sensitivity chart showing the sensitivity of the output to the ranges in the inputs

If you do not want to run a simulation, you can end run the issue by just plugging in the highest and lowest values for each assumption into the spreadsheet and record the impact on the output. You can then generate a table showing the impact on performance as each assumption takes on its highest and lowest values. This provides some insight but it lacks the depth of a simulation which takes into account correlations between assumptions, meaning that some might be at the high end of their range while others are at the low end of their range. A Monte Carlo simulation tests all possible assumption values by running thousands of iterations of the financial model to provide a rather complete look at the range of outcomes that can be expected. The goal is to derive a list of about seven to ten assumptions where you can least afford to be wrong. These are the places to focus your CheckPoint planning and creatively engineer your opportunity.

Table 3.7 shows that sensitivity analyses carried out by the Office Desk team identified that there were nine assumptions that were most critical to profits; the other assumptions had much less of an effect.

A simulation was also used to determine the sensitivity of the project ROA to changes in the assumptions that yielded what we call a *staircase chart*, shown in Figure 3.3. As you can see, whatever sensitivity approach you use, only a few assumptions are critical to profits (see Table 3.7) or ROA (see Figure 3.3).

TABLE 3.7   Sensitivity Analysis of Office Desk Project Profits

Assumption	Effect of Lowest Value on Profits	Effect of Highest Value on Profits	Assumption Number
Desks per Order	–51%	+22%	6
Sales Calls per Day	–20%	+12%	8
Wholesale Price of Desk	–20%	+23%	4
Raw Materials Cost	+23%	–19%	12
Advertising Percent of Sales	+12%	–16%	5
Sales Commissions	+12%	–12%	10
Salesperson Salary	+5%	–9%	11
Equipment Cost per Line	+10%	–9%	18
Sales Calls per Order	–7%	+13%	7

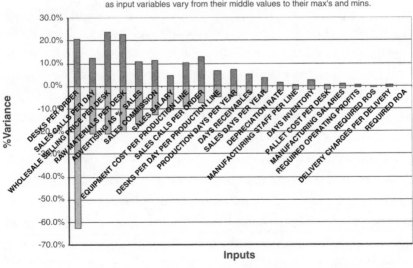

Staircase Chart

Illustrates Volatility: Shows contribution to upside and downside of output variable, as input variables vary from their middle values to their max's and mins.

■ Downside Case   ■ Upside Case

Figure 3.3   Staircase chart showing ROA sensitivities

Sensitivity analysis brings us to the end of stage one of OE. It has given us a DDP, which frames the challenges, a set of assumptions that underpin the project's prospects, and from the sensitivity analysis, the list of those key variables where the project's performance is most vulnerable to error. In the next chapter, we turn to CheckPointing, which looks at using OE concepts for systematically structuring your investment in order to increase reach and eradicate major risk.

Appendix: More on the Consumption Chain

The following is a brief overview of the Consumption Chain. Those readers who want to learn more should read *The Entrepreneurial Mindset* by Rita Gunther McGrath and Ian C. MacMillan, Harvard Business School Press, 2000.

The Consumption Chain breaks down the typical customer experience with a product or service into several steps, beginning with an emerging *awareness of need* on the customer's part. With consumers, this first step may be caused by a variety of inputs that signal that something is needed, whether it be the need for a new car, the desire for a vacation, a retirement, or some other event. Amazon has come up with a clever way to trigger an "awareness of need" by providing purchasers with a list of books that relate to the one being purchased. After a customer realizes the need for something, the next step in the Consumption Chain is the *search for a solution* that satisfies that need. Google is an obvious example of a company that has differentiated itself at this step of the Consumption Chain. What is interesting about Google is its capability to make its service ubiquitous and, at this point, indispensable to both business customers and consumers searching for anything and everything.

After a customer has found an appropriate solution to the need, the next step in the progression is the *selection* of a product or service that meets the customer's criteria. Strategic differentiation stems from thinking deeply about how it might be possible to help your customer make a decision about the purchase. To understand the customer experience, we use questions such as what are customers doing *when* they select a product or service, *where* are they, *who* are they with or who would they like to be with in an ideal world, and *why* are they making a purchase to help managers parse out a winning strategy.

After selection, the next step is *ordering/purchasing* the item or service. Amazon comes to mind with its early and continuing differentiating feature of the shopping cart that stores information about customer preferences and payment methods to make it simple to purchase items.

Financing the purchase forms the next step of the chain, and this provides companies that have strong balance sheets a way to differentiate themselves by selling a solution rather than a product that forms part of the solution. In the consumer markets, the auto companies have been doing this for a long time, with their low-cost leases that require customers to pay for only the part of the car that they will actually use during the term of the lease rather than basing payments on the full purchase price. In the industrial space, K & F Industries, Inc. sells its brake systems for commercial aircraft at a loss when a new airframe enters the market, with the intention of making a profit on replacement parts. As a result, the company is basically linking the cost of its product to the revenue stream of its customers in that the number of times an aircraft lands relates directly to the replacement cycle of its brake systems.

The *payment* of purchases of less-costly items and services can provide a way for companies to differentiate themselves. With its speed pass, Exxon, for example, allows customers to simply swipe the electronic purse in front of its gas pumps or cash registers to pay for fuel or food items at its service stations. Although this feature of its service stations might not be of earth-shaking value to well-heeled customers, it is a differentiating benefit to teenage drivers who lack credit cards and those without bank accounts.

The next link in the chain is *tracking/receiving* an item that was purchased. UPS has differentiated its delivery service by providing customers with up-to-the-minute e-mails that chronicle every step of the delivery process, from the time that their package was picked up to the time that the delivery was completed. With this service, it is no longer necessary to manually track a delivery on the company's website because the system informs customers automatically.

Installation provides ways for companies to differentiate themselves. Home Depot and Lowe's have adopted this step for differentiation by following the aging demographics of their customers and offering them certified installation experts who can do the work for an additional fee.

Storing and moving is sometimes the next step in the chain. One company, PODS, created a differentiation strategy with its delivery and storage system that offers the convenience of containerized shipping to consumers, small businesses, and government organizations. Rather than load items for transport or long-term storage into a truck that requires that they be handled at least twice, once loading and then again at unloading, PODS delivers a container to the customer's location. Customers load their contents into the container that sits at ground level, adding to the convenience, and the container is then picked up using a patented loading system that places the container onto its truck for transport to a delivery destination or to its company's warehouse for storage. This disaggregation of the moving and storage service created an enormous opportunity for the company, and it was the result of thinking deeply about the customer experience at this point in the consumption chain.

After installing or storing a purchase, customers *use* a product. Industrial companies that sell intermediate products to businesses often send in engineers to make sure that their component products are used in the most effective way, to ensure repeat business. Apple, in addition to its design differentiation, focuses on this step by making the integration of its equipment with peripherals seamless from the users' point of view.

Repairs and returns can sometimes be the next step in the chain. In the consumer space, prompt and effortless returns is expected from most merchants at this point, but Zappos.com, an online shoe store, has made that a basic part of its message. Shoes obviously require an exact fit, so its online purchase has always presented a challenge. Zappos.com offers free shipping and returns to encourage customers to try buying online. Its policy also encourages customers to order several pairs of shoes with the intention of returning all but one, which mimics the experience of going into a shoe store.

Companies that sell any sort of complex product, or service, usually focus on the *service* link in the chain as a way to differentiate themselves. The Harris Corporation sells a technology to jet engine manufacturers that allows, through ground link technology, for real-time monitoring of engine performance during flights. This enables engine manufacturers to recommend needed maintenance to their airline customers between scheduled service intervals if it is needed, providing a service link to its product that is hard for competitors to disrupt.

The last link in the Consumption Chain is *disposal* of a product. In the near past, this step was often overlooked, but with increased environmental awareness product disposal has become an issue that bears attention. As companies seek out a green image by focusing on how their products, or their suppliers' products, can be recycled, this link has become a hot topic. The Patagonia clothing manufacturer has taken the lead by offering to take back certain types of its used clothing from its customers so that the fibers can be recycled into entirely new garments made by the company.

Service Businesses

Although the Consumption Chain is presented here in a fashion that relates directly to physical products, our experience is that it is equally useful when used with services. It is a shorter chain when used with services, but the key links remain. In a service context, we begin always with the awareness of need, which is followed by a search for a solution. The next link, selection, certainly applies, as does the purchasing link. Some services may include an opportunity for differentiation at the financing and paying links if the service is costly. Take, for example, the practice of doctors providing financing for cosmetic surgery through third-party providers. In a similar fashion, commercial insurance policies can be very expensive, and some insurance companies provide for financing the policy to make the purchase decision easier for customers. The receiving and servicing links apply to the insurance industry where agents deliver the physical policy to the customer. Chubb Insurance, for example, differentiates itself by its claims department, which provides the same functions as a physical service department for products, managing customer expectations when they have a problem.

4

How to Engineer Opportunities, Stage 2: CheckPointing

Structuring Your Approach to Ramping Up Your Reach and Eradicating Your Risk

In this chapter, we show you how to carry out the second major stage of the Opportunity Engineering (OE) process to engineer an investment opportunity. (The first was Discovery Driven Planning [DDP].) CheckPointing comprises two parts:

1. Opportunity Engineering charting, which systematically maps Opportunity Engineering moves you develop to reduce risk and increase reach

2. Generating a CheckPoint/Assumption Table, which systematically documents all the places you will be testing assumptions ahead of investment

As in previous chapters, we use a highly simplified example of an actual case, but again the same logic can be applied to the more complex projects that you face in your business.

CheckPoints are test events that you deliberately design into the plan that enable you to test assumptions as the plan unfolds. It is important to recognize that every CheckPoint in a DDP is a planned *event* at which you will observe some completed outcome. It is not a date or the start of an activity.

Let's look at the two parts of the CheckPointing process a bit more closely:

1. *Identify Engineering Opportunities* to increase reach and reduce risk. You need to review your DDP to identify all the major investments and resource commitments implied by the DDP and creatively develop engineered calls, engineered puts, and other engineering moves that increase upside reach or pare away downside risk. You build these moves into an Opportunity Engineering chart that identifies all the Opportunity Engineering CheckPoints for your project. These Opportunity Engineering moves provide the first CheckPoints to be entered into the CheckPoint/assumption table.

2. *Identify additional CheckPoints* designed to test your key assumptions from the DDP and add these into the CheckPoint/assumption table. Here you create CheckPoints to deliberately design ways of testing the assumptions you generated in the DDP. As the project unfolds, at each CheckPoint you adjust the ranges of your assumptions ahead of major resource commitments, and on the basis of these updated assumptions, you replan, redirect, or stop the project in the light of the new information yielded by the CheckPoint test.

As you assemble your CheckPoints, you systematically document which assumptions you will be testing in a CheckPoint/Assumption Table, like Table 4.1, in which the assumptions to be tested at each CheckPoint are clearly specified. You should also specify who is responsible for making sure that relevant assumptions are revisited at that CheckPoint. No assumption should go untested, and critical assumptions should be tested as many times and in as many ways as your creativity can generate!

TABLE 4.1   CheckPoint/Assumption Table

CheckPoint #	CheckPoint Name	Assumptions to Be Tested	Cost to Complete CheckPoint	Person Responsible for CheckPoint

We use two examples to illustrate the CheckPointing process. First, we revisit the Office Desk case from the preceding chapter. Then we consider a more complex case of a company that was doing research on a new Tasmanian Devil product that differed from its traditional mass volume chemical products, and was therefore facing considerable uncertainty surrounding both its capability to produce the product and the market surrounding it.

In this chapter, we concentrate only on showing you how to use CheckPointing to Opportunity Engineer and create value in projects. In Chapter 7, "Project Valuation Using EVS Software," we describe in detail how to use our Engineered Value Solver (EVS) software for project valuation.

Note, however, that if you want to use your own valuation methodology, you can use the concepts in this chapter without ever using our EVS valuation software. The actual valuation is very useful, but it is the dessert, not the main meal. The OE thought process is where the value lies.

Identifying Engineering Opportunities to Increase Reach and Reduce Risk

The first step in CheckPointing is to review the reverse income statements and balance sheets and identify all major investment requirements and fixed-cost commitments. Then you need to push your team to help you think of creative ways to engineer the project (for instance, by designing multiple stages of resource commitment and by building in engineered puts, engineered calls, and engineered abandonments).

We have found a systematic way of doing this, which is to subject each major resource commitment to a "Catechism" (the OE Catechism). In other words, for each major resource commitment, ask the following:

1. Can you postpone investment until a time when a major uncertainty will be resolved (e.g., pending legislation, litigation outcome, technology breakthrough, new market opening up)? Remember, however, that any such delays should not compromise the investment's competitive potential or render it obsolete!

2. Can you increase flexibility of decision making? (For example, can you stage the investment or resource commitment, can you find alternative customers or uses if some don't work out, or can you follow an alternative technical development path if the first does not work out?)

3. Can you create tests to probe and reduce the uncertainties surrounding the investment? (For example, can you use market tests to probe new markets or develop early, less-challenging applications that allow you to learn your way in to a new technology development?)

4. Can you create engineered calls, namely smaller, experimental investments that provide information that gives you the right, but not the obligation, to proceed further?

5. Can you find ways to recoup on the investment if the project fails to deliver on expectations? (That is, can you engineer abandonment value?)

6. Can you create a way to put disappointments to someone else? In other words, can you find ways for other parties (other firms, potential suppliers, distributors or customers, government agencies, other organizations) to absorb part or all of the costs if you fail?

Office Desk Revisited

We now illustrate CheckPointing by revisiting the Office Desk case and show how the team developed Engineered Opportunities for their desk project and then created a CheckPoint/assumption table.

Step 1: Identify Engineering Opportunities and Build CheckPointing Charts for the Initial CheckPoint / Assumption Table

The place to start is by revisiting the reverse balance sheet, the reverse income statement, and the CheckPoint/Assumption Table and identify major resource commitments that will be needed. The reverse balance sheet in Figure 3.5 (in Chapter 3, "How to Engineer Opportunities, Stage 1: DDP") showed commitments of about $6 million for equipment, $6 million for receivables, and $2 million for inventory. The Office Desk team quickly decided that receivables and the inventory could be ramped up slowly as the business grew so that only successful progress would allow them to earn the right to these substantial commitments. However, there remained the cost of equipment. The team needed to engineer a way of testing the market's appetite for the desk before building a plant.

They started the OEP process by creating a "pre-engineering" CheckPointing chart in Figure 4.1a, which calls for an investment of $6 million in equipment that would hopefully yield total profits of $6.3 million over six years.

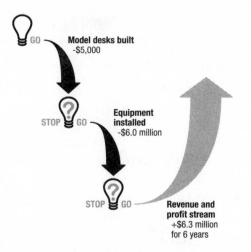

Figure 4.1a   Office Desk OEP chart: Raw project

The EVS software yields the following valuation components:

NPVe = Net present value engineered

OV = Opportunity value

AV = Abandonment value

EV = The total Engineered Value, the sum of the preceding value
components (and thus the most important)

Using our EVS software, the value components of Office Desk
from Figure 4.1a come to this:

NPVe = –$1.93 million

OV = 0

AV = 0

EV = –$1.93 million

With a large negative NPV like this, the project would be considered dead on arrival in most companies.

However, once the team started to catechize this plant expenditure, two engineering moves quickly came to mind, as illustrated in Figure 4.1b:

Engineering Opportunity 1: Spend $15,000 to build several models of the desk and use these models to do several market studies, which would allow the team to

- Conduct focus group studies using the model with distributors and future customers.
- Recruit beta users to try the model desks.
- Complete focus group studies with these beta users.
- Test the trial models with high-end distributors.

The $50,000 estimated cost of these studies, coupled with the $15,000 for model desks, in effect created a $65,000 engineered call on the future profit streams but also significantly reduced the risk of having to write off $6 million of plant equipment.

Engineering Opportunity 2: By buying more general-purpose *resalable* equipment (and losing somewhat on efficiency), they could engineer in AV by selling the equipment for $1.5 million if the project failed.

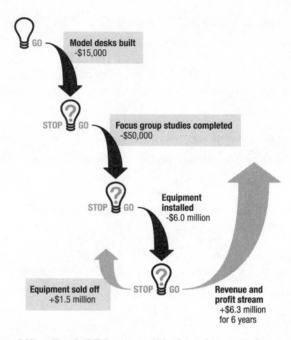

Figure 4.1b   Office Desk OEP chart: AV of equipment plus engineered call via focus group study

Note that many of these ideas are routinely carried out by smart firms, **BUT SELDOM ARE THESE ENGINEERING MOVES FORMALLY ADDRESSED AND INCLUDED IN THE VALUATION**.

Our approach differs in that it encourages managers to really think through how to change the risk reward profile of a project, as each major investment or fixed cost is planned, by finding ways to mitigate the downside exposure and then including these engineering moves in the valuation.

These basic changes to the development plan as illustrated in Figure 4.1b had the significant effect on project value, as shown here:

$$NPVe = -\$0.93 \text{ million}$$

$$OV = \$2.09 \text{ million}$$

$$AV = \$0.51 \text{ million}$$

$$EV = \$0.84 \text{ million}$$

What caused the values to shift? By spending $15,000 on building model desks for focus group studies, they were able to address some of the market uncertainty. Thus, they built a CheckPoint at which some of the market-related assumptions could be tested. This provided an exit point, and a low-cost one at that. If the market information was not supportive of the project, the effort could be redirected or terminated. The effect of this CheckPoint is seen in the 50% reduction in the negative NPV and the creation of $2.09 million of OV. The change in equipment specifications to multipurpose machinery created AV because the equipment could be sold off if necessary.

The AV is roughly a third of the $1.5 million sell-off price because we are valuing the *opportunity to sell* the equipment, rather than a projected sale price.

Engineering Opportunities 3 and 4: Next, two engineered calls emerged when the team began catechizing how to test the several critical assumptions associated with selling the desks without building a plant (highlighted in Figure 4.1c).

They began engineering by coming up with the idea of subcontracting the production of a batch of 1,000 desks to an existing molding firm. This would address Office Desk's unfamiliarity with the production process. Following on this, to reduce the market uncertainty, the Office Desk team decided to try to subcontract the sales of these desks through an office furniture manufacturers' representative firm (rep firm), which would include the sample desks in their line of offerings: Office Desk would try to cut a deal with the rep firm to work closely with their salespeople, thus letting the salespeople track the sales reps' experience in trying to sell the new product. This would allow Office Desk to generate more accurate estimates of critical assumptions, such as desks per order, sales calls, price, and sales calls per order. This mapped onto the revised OEP chart shown in Figure 4.1c.

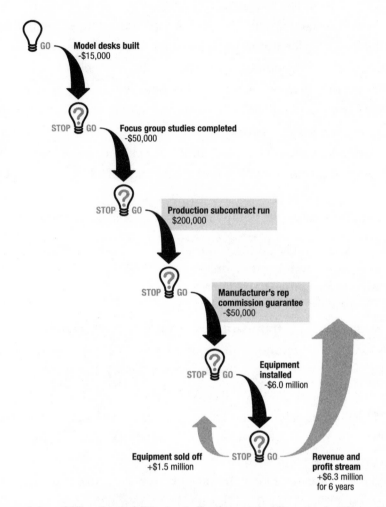

Figure 4.1c   Office Desk OEP chart: Engineered calls - production sub-contract and manufacturers' representative sales

The cost, including the cost of a mold, to produce a batch of 1,000 desks was estimated at about $200 per desk, so $200,000 was needed to build the test batch. The rep firm was willing to market this test batch of desks at $300+ per desk for a commission of 33% but were asking for a guaranteed total commission of $50,000 to be paid in advance. The $250,000 required by these two moves, in effect, created an engineered call on the $6.3 million of future revenues and provided a CheckPoint for eschewing investment in plant if the test batch threw these projections into question. The value of this $250,000 expenditure simply cannot be captured using conventional financial metrics, but it is captured using the EVS software. This additional OEP changed the value of the project for the better, as shown here:

NPVe = $0.19 million

OV = $1.01 million

AV = $0.12 million

EV = $1.31 million

Engineering Opportunity 5: Next, the team looked at engineering the $250,000 cost of these two engineered calls (see Figure 4.1d) by creating AV. The first opportunity was to recognize that even if the desk failed miserably in this pilot program, the unsold desks would have a fire-sale AV estimated at $30,000. But then the team really got creative and proposed an engineered put to the manufacturers' rep that went as follows: "If you commit to paying us $150,000 for all the desks, irrespective of sales and price, and let us work with your sales force to get the data we need, you then keep all revenues from sales of all the desks." This meant that the rep firm would be getting 1,000 desks, with a potential selling price of $300+ per desk, for only $150 dollars per desk—less than the direct cost of the desk.

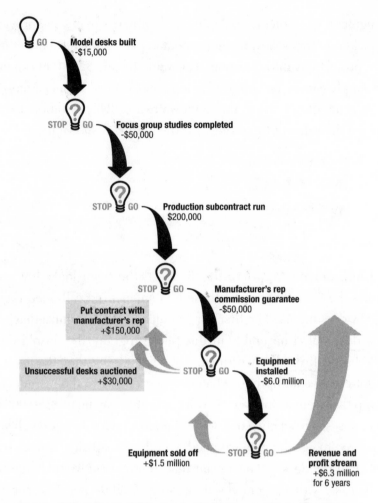

Figure 4.1d   Office Desk OEP chart: AV from unsold desks plus engineered put proposal

By adding these two steps to the project plan, which provided further options for managing the uncertainties surrounding the project, the value shifted up again:

$$NPVe = \$0.35 \text{ million}$$

$$OV = \$1.02 \text{ million}$$

$$AV = \$0.29 \text{ million}$$

$$EV = \$1.67 \text{ million}$$

Engineering Opportunity 6: The team was still uncomfortable with a commitment of $6 million for a full-scale plant. Figure 4.1e shows how they created a final engineered call: They decided that if the rep sales went well, they could build a prototype production line, with primarily general-purpose machinery, for $1.5 million, and use this prototype line to learn how to produce desks at the lowest cost before building a full-scale plant. Large parts of this prototype line could be sold off as secondhand general-purpose equipment for $500,000 if the project were discontinued, creating AV. In addition, the capacity of the prototype line could be used for later full-scale production, thereby reducing the investment in the final plant from the $6 million level to $5 million, for a total investment in plant of $6.5 million.

Even though the equipment cost increased to a total of $6.5 million (including the $1.5 million prototype line), the effect of adding more choices for management and breaking down the equipment investment into two parts increased project values even further:

$$NPVe = \$0.41 \text{ million}$$
$$OV = \$0.96 \text{ million}$$
$$AV = \$0.44 \text{ million}$$
$$EV = \$1.81 \text{ million}$$

The Office Desk case was one of our more interesting engineered cases. A project that started off "dead in the water" with a value of negative $1.93 million was engineered into an opportunity valued at $1.81 million!

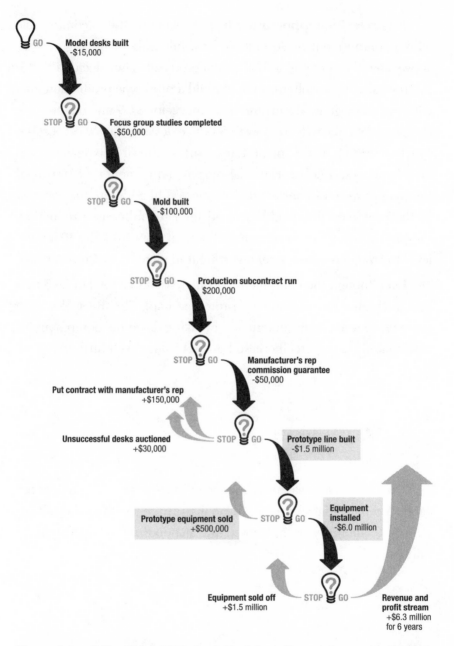

Model desks built
-$15,000

Focus group studies completed
-$50,000

Mold built
-$100,000

Production subcontract run
$200,000

Manufacturer's rep
commission guarantee
-$50,000

Put contract with manufacturer's rep
+$150,000

Unsuccessful desks auctioned
+$30,000

Prototype line built
-$1.5 million

Prototype equipment sold
+$500,000

Equipment
installed
-$6.0 million

Equipment sold off
+$1.5 million

Revenue and
profit stream
+$6.3 million
for 6 years

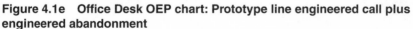

Figure 4.1e   Office Desk OEP chart: Prototype line engineered call plus engineered abandonment

With the OEP completed, we next begin filling out a Check-Point/Assumption Table that reflects all CheckPoints generated by the final OEP chart, as we have done in Table 4.2. (At this stage, we have not filled out which assumptions will be tested. That is done only after identifying CheckPoints to test critical assumptions—Step 2 of the process.)

TABLE 4.2   Initial CheckPoint/Assumption Table for the Office Desk Project

CheckPoint Number	CheckPoint Event	Assumptions Tested	Cost
1	Model desks produced		$15K
2	Focus groups studies with distributors done		$25K
3	Focus group study with user groups finished		$25K
4	Production subcontract run		$200K
5	Manufacturer's rep contract completed		$50K
6	Manufacturer's rep purchased unsold desks		$150K
7	Prototype line built		$1.5M
8	Prototype line sold		–$500K
9	Full plant installed		$5.0M
10	Equipment sold off		–$1.5 M

Identify Additional CheckPoints to Test Key Assumptions

Key assumption CheckPoints are specific events that you design in to allow you to test your key assumptions and thereby progressively reduce the ranges of your initial assumptions as the CheckPoints unfold. As you progress from early to later CheckPoints, you will build increasing confidence in the revised assumption numbers that emerge from your tests, thereby reducing the risk of the investment. So, you plan your CheckPoints in ways that let you carry out low-cost tests early in the development process, with the purpose of inexpensively reducing the range of your estimates for the key assumptions, not necessarily confirming them in the beginning but allowing you to narrow their spread. As you move from early to later CheckPoints, this should result in a reduction in overall project uncertainty and thus justify increased increments of investment.

Typical CheckPoint outcomes that allow you to test assumptions for products include completed market studies, pilot plant operation, prototype developed and market tested, and trial sales program completed. Other kinds of projects, such as services or financial or software or technology development, will have their own specific types of CheckPoints that are appropriate, (e.g., prototype system developed, prototype system tested, operating system test completed, and software segment debugged).

Note again that the exemplar CheckPoints previously mentioned all denote something completed, not initiated. The completed event list lets you review your list of assumptions and ask which might be tested or probed at each CheckPoint so that you can plan ahead of time to do this testing. Particularly for the most critical assumptions from your staircase chart or sensitivity analysis, you need to be sure that before making major resource commitments you have designed CheckPoints for testing them, preferably several CheckPoints for the most critical assumptions.

In the spirit of "failing fast, failing cheap, and moving on," we have found that it can be very useful if you can think up ways of creating early "tripwire" CheckPoints, which are *designed to show you are wrong* in the early stages. Such "planning to fail" seems antithetical to traditional management thinking, but it is the essence OEP thinking: that if there is no future in the project, learn this quickly and inexpensively. It prevents a lot of downstream waste and anguish.

The sensitivity analysis identified most critical assumptions—those that most impact the profitability and profit projections. The objective is to design CheckPoints that will enable you to test these assumptions ahead of major resource commitments.

The most critical variables for Office Desk were identified in Chapter 3 and are repeated in Table 4.3.

TABLE 4.3   High Profit Impact Variables (from Figure 3.7)

Assumption	Effect of Lowest Value on Profits	Effect of Highest Value on Profits	Assumption Number
Desks per order	–51%	+22%	6
Sales calls per day	–20%	+12%	8
Wholesale price of desk	–20%	+23%	4
Raw materials cost	+23%	–19%	12
Advertising percent of sales	+12%	–16%	5
Sales commissions	+12%	–12%	10
Salesperson salary	+5%	–9%	11
Equipment cost per line	+10%	–9%	18
Sales calls per order	–7%	+13%	7

So, the challenge is to design CheckPoints for testing these assumptions ahead of a major investment. For the Office Desk team, the first CheckPoints were relatively straightforward:

- Complete a detailed market study.
- Complete a feasibility analysis.
- Conduct and finish a nationwide market research project.
- Recruit and train the sales and production staff.
- Install the production equipment.
- Produce a consignment of desks to go to major distributors.

Adding these CheckPoints to the list from Table 4.2 enabled the team to generate an assumption/CheckPoint Table like 4.4, where they systematically listed all the assumptions they would be testing at each CheckPoint. Using the insights from the DDP, they also estimated the cost of each CheckPoint.

Table 4.4 Final CheckPoint/Assumption Table for Office Desk Project

CheckPoint Number	CheckPoint Event	Assumption Tested	Cost
1	Market study completed	4, 5, 6–11,	$10K
2	Feasibility study done	1–3, 4, 5, 6–11, 18, 19	$15K
3	Model desks produced	1–3, 4, 12,13, 14–17,18,19	$15K
4	Focus groups studies with distributors done	4, 5, 6–11, 20–22	$15K
5	Focus group study with user groups finished	4, 5, 6–11	$25K
6	Full-scale market research completed	1, 2, 3, 4, 5, 6–11	$50K
7	Trial model beta users recruited	1, 2, 3, 4, 5, 6–11	$10K
8	Focus group discussions with beta users ended	1, 2, 3, 4, 5, 6–11	$25K
9	Trial models with high-end distributors tested	1–3, 4, 5, 6–11, 18, 19, 20–22	$20K
10	Production subcontract run	12–19	$200K
11	Contract sales by manufacturer's representative done	1–11, 20–22	$50K
12	Manufacturer's rep purchased unsold desks		$100K
13	Prototype production line installed	1–3, 12,13, 14–17,18,19	$1.5M
14	Recruitment and training of pilot production staff finished	16–19	$100K
15	Recruitment and training pilot sales staff done	10–11	$150K
16	Inventory for consignments to prime distributors dispatched	20–22	$500K
17	Prototype line sold for abandonment value		–$500K
18	Full production plant commissioned	12–20	$5.0M
19	Marketing campaign completed	1–4	$500K
20	Equipment sold off for abandonment value		–$1.5 M

The team carefully thought through which assumptions could be tested at each CheckPoint so that they would avoid regretting not having tested an assumption when they had the chance. Note that if they follow the initial program laid out in Table 4.4, all assumptions will be tested at least once, and the most critical assumptions will be tested several times. Finally, in the far-right column, the Office Desk team made estimates of what it would cost to accomplish each CheckPoint.

Table 4.4 lists the expanded set of CheckPoints and their associated assumptions that emerged from the CheckPointing exercise. As you can see, the table starts with inexpensive CheckPoints designed to narrow the uncertainty range for assumptions at low cost. This is what makes OE a plan to learn—you learn your way to the real opportunity, redirecting (or even discontinuing if necessary) at each CheckPoint. As the project moves to each successive CheckPoint, the ranges of assumptions need to decrease, demonstrating increasing confidence in the unfolding reality, which justifies increasing increments in investment.

In conclusion, Opportunity Engineering and its catechizing questions is a great vehicle for focusing on creative ways to decrease risk by avoiding major investments and fixed-cost commitments until the uncertainty surrounding a project has been reduced, by testing the major assumptions using the assumption/CheckPoint table to organize and track the effort.

Plan Execution

After (and only after) you have developed a DDP that is looking like it will deliver to its scope specification and you have engineered out the major risk should you develop the more detailed project plan. This plan will be needed to specify how to get from where you are now (with no staff, no equipment, no funds, no customers, no revenues!) to where you hope to be in the six-year time horizon. Only then should you put in the significant effort it takes to do first-cut five-year budgets, capital plans, staffing plans, and so on. Once again, because the plan is uncertain, and probably wrong, there is little point in going into great detail, *because your job is to learn from the unfolding development effort and keep redirecting to create the true opportunity.* You need enough detail to have an idea what funds and staff are likely to be needed, so we usually put together annual budgets and staffing estimates, perhaps with a quarterly budget for the first year.

More important than trying to be right is the willingness to *replan* at every major CheckPoint. Chances are, you will be wrong, at least about some things; so at each CheckPoint, decide how to redirect in the light of new knowledge *or shut down*. The dictum is this: If you are going to fail, fail fast, fail cheap, and move on to the next opportunity.

Therefore, we suggest, as we did to the team in the Office Desk project, that you follow the 15x30 rule. Do not have more than 30 major assumptions to check, and do not have more than 15 CheckPoints. Why? Any more than this and you will more than likely never replan— it is too time-consuming and painful.

This concludes the Office Desk CheckPointing example. In the next section, we will take you through a somewhat more complex charting process (but not the CheckPoint/assumption table). If you are comfortable with the idea of Opportunity Engineering charting, feel free to skip to the next chapter.

Case 2: Opportunity Engineering Charting: Tasmanian Devil Project

If you are still unclear on the Opportunity Engineering charting process, we take you through another case called the Tasmanian Devil project. It is named after the Looney Tunes character that ate everything in its path, which is what the new halogen molecule of our exemplar company appeared to do. The firm had discovered a highly corrosive, halogen-based molecule that could dissolve almost any ceramic much more effectively and more precisely than existing compounds.

The plan was to see whether this Tasmanian Devil molecule could be developed to deliver a product and process for etching or otherwise cutting ceramic products with molecular precision.

We go straight to identifying Engineering Opportunities and Opportunity Engineering charting.

Identify Major Investment or Fixed-Cost Commitments and Use Catechizing to Identify Engineering Opportunities

The Tasmanian Devil team had identified the following major estimated investments:

1. Total R&D cost for development of the Tasmanian Devil product from test tube to operating pilot plant of $700,000—but with a range between $600,000 and $900,000.

2. Installation of a plant to produce Tasmanian Devil—estimated at $4.5 million, but the estimate ranged between $4 million and $7 million.

Their DDP indicated that the profits per year depended on whether they could get a patent in two years:

• With the patent, profits would be $4 million per year (standard deviation $1.5 million) with ten years from launch to competitive erosion of profits.

• Without the patent, profits would be $3 million per year (standard deviation $1.5 million) with four years from launch to erosion of profits.

So, the Tasmanian Devil team had the choice of going for patenting (thus delaying the project) or "going naked" by building a plant without IP protection.

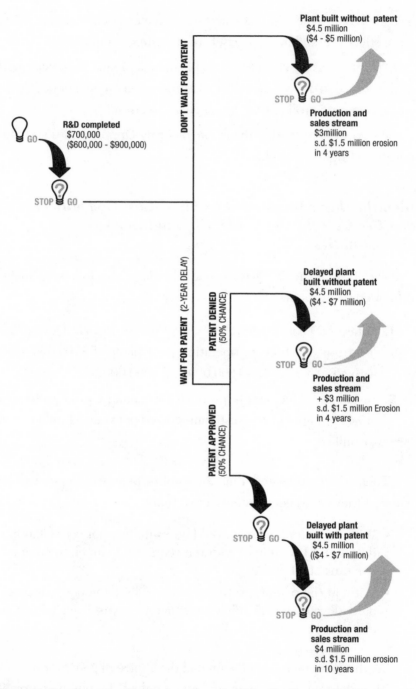

Figure 4.2a   Opportunity Engineering chart for the Tasmanian Devil project: Pre-engineering

The first version of the Opportunity Engineering chart looked like Figure 4.2a. Once R&D is completed, there are three possibilities going forward:

1. Apply for a patent, causing delayed plant construction while the patent approval is awaited, but which if approved yields a high but delayed profit stream.

2. Apply for a patent, causing delayed plant construction while the patent approval is awaited, and which if *not* approved yields a reduced and delayed profit stream due to competitive matching.

3. "Go naked" and build without a patent, thus speeding up the time to generate profits, but suffering from earlier competitive matching.

Note that because this is a more complex opportunity than the Office Desk case, in Figure 4.2a we have included data from their DDP that reflects the uncertainties. So, for instance, the R&D is shown as estimated at most likely cost $700,000, lowest cost $600,000, and highest $900,000. Furthermore, the annual revenue generated if the plant is patented is shown in Figure 4.2a as $4 million, with a standard deviation of $1.5 million, running for 10 years before competitive erosion.

Engineering Opportunity 1: Two-stage R&D. The first stage of the product development of the new Tasmanian Devil product calls for R&D in the lab at an expected cost of $600,000 to $900,000. The question is whether there is the possibility to engineer this portion of the product development effort to increase the return profile of the project. This is depicted in Figure 4.2b.

They decided that the project could be broken into the two stages depicted in Figure 4.2b. The first stage was to develop a batch process for producing the molecule, costing $400,000, which would lead to a follow-on investment of $300,000 if it produced encouraging results, or the research could be curtailed.

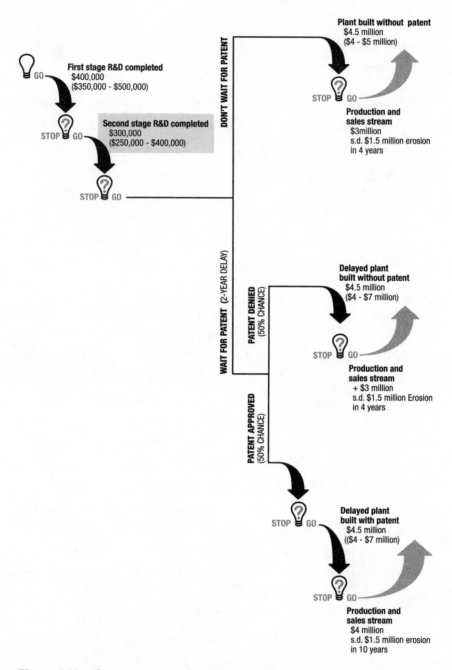

Figure 4.2b   Opportunity Engineering chart for the Tasmanian Devil project: Two-stage R&D

Breaking down the R&D into two or more stages starts to engineer the results because the same upside potential exists, but the project could be stopped after spending just the first $400,000. If key uncertainties could be answered by spending less, the return profile would be even better.[1] Importantly, all we have done so far is just think differently about the R&D effort. Thinking differently is the essence of OE.

Engineering Opportunity 2: Test market. Because the R&D effort was successful, the next step the Tasmanian Devil team engineered was to test market the Tasmanian Devil product to make sure that it met the needs of the targeted customers. This is charted in Figure 4.2c.

Engineering Opportunity 3: Pilot production plant. The cost of the plant is expected to be $4.5 million. But management concedes that they have never built a plant of this nature and that the cost could vary from $4 to $7 million. Figure 4.2d shows how they decided to include a pilot production plant to test assumptions regarding the cost of the plant, its efficiency, and its actual production capacity.

Engineering Opportunity 4: Sell IP. Next, the Tasmanian Devil team explored the possibility of selling IP if the original market did not pan out as hoped. Sale of IP creates AV. Figure 4.2e shows that if the patent is pursued and approved, there is abandonment opportunity in selling the IP should the project be discontinued before the plant is built.

---

[1] The R&D effort from Stage 1 may produce intellectual property (IP) that could be sold to another company, so there could be AV associated with the R&D. The caveat is that the company must be open to the possibility of selling IP to create AV, if that becomes the best path forward. Think of it as though the AV were subtracted from the cost of the R&D. Therefore, the downside risk of a loss has been reduced, while the potential upside remains the same, increasing the asymmetric return.

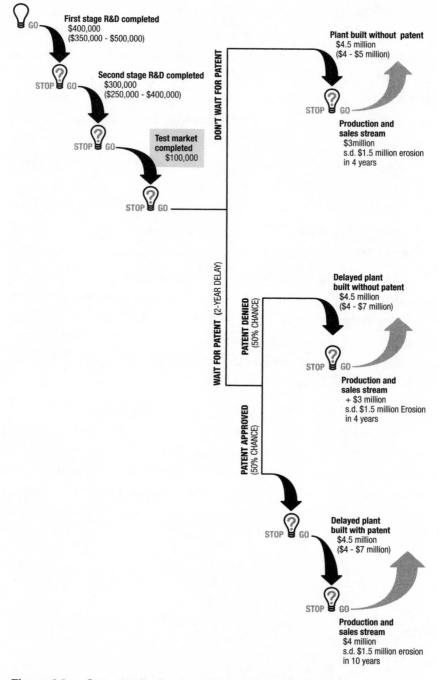

Figure 4.2c   Opportunity Engineering chart for the Tasmanian Devil project: Market test call

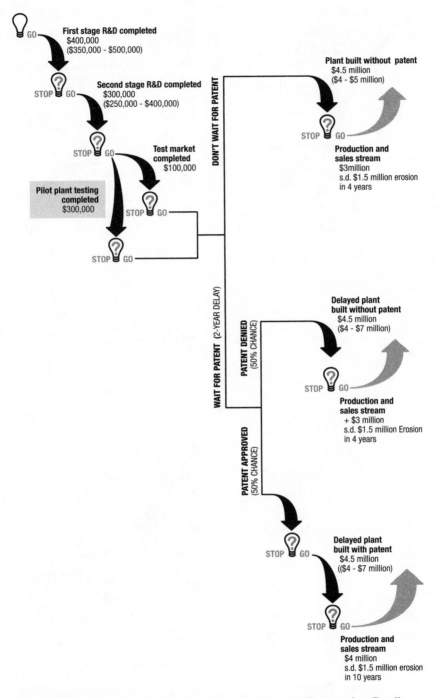

Figure 4.2d   Opportunity Engineering chart for the Tasmanian Devil project: Pilot plant call

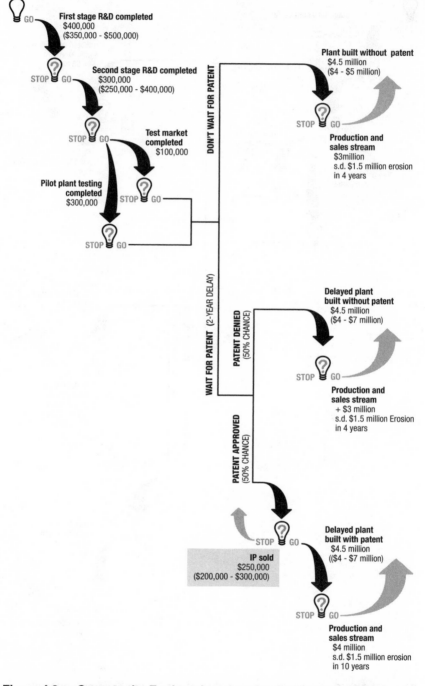

Figure 4.2e   Opportunity Engineering chart for the Tasmanian Devil project: Sale of IP

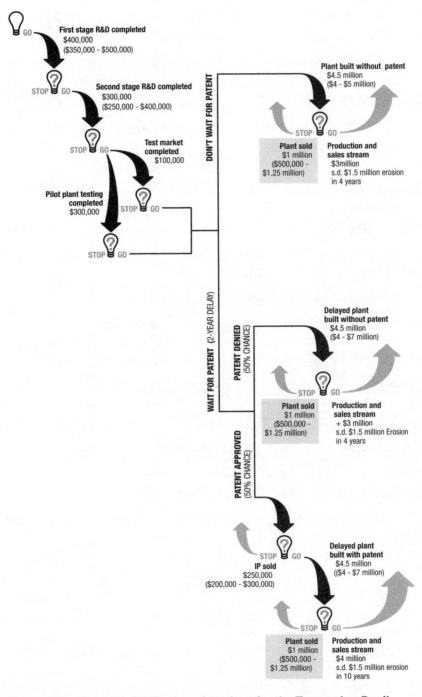

Figure 4.2f   Opportunity Engineering chart for the Tasmanian Devil project: Pilot plant call

Engineering Opportunity 5: Sell plant. Figure 4.2f shows the team's realization that even if the project melted down, the plant could be dismantled and the equipment and land resold, with or without the IP. The discerning factor in valuing this option to abandon is the price that the plant might fetch on the market, which is directly affected by the plant's design. For example, a plant that can be refitted to produce several types of products is more valuable than a plant that is limited to producing one product. The logic is simple: A plant that can serve many purposes can appeal to a wider array of buyers. The logic is used by Japanese auto manufacturers that build plants to allow production of several of their vehicles, as opposed to Ford, which had to mothball a large plant because it could be used to build only the Taurus, which was eventually dropped from its lineup.

In this example, we tried to illustrate how the value of a project is substantially different from what is typically captured by traditional financial metrics that are based on a linear path from beginning to end. Each stage of development offers the capability to change the return profile of a project just by thinking about it in a different manner using OE. In Chapter 7, we return to this example and show how to use the EVS software to calculate how the value of a project evolves as the development moves from R&D to production.

This concludes the CheckPointing chapter. In the next chapter, we look at another issue that influences decisions to invest in uncertain, high-potential projects: how to build a portfolio of several such projects.

5

Creating an Engineered Growth Portfolio

Most successful companies build an Engineered Growth Portfolio of investments—some that are basic/core investments, some that offer new growth opportunities, and some that are high-potential long shots. In this chapter, we look at using Opportunity Engineering as a tool you can use in building an engineered growth portfolio of investments.

Innovation requires the resolution of two main sources of uncertainty.[1] The first involves the *Internal Challenges* a company faces in trying to develop new products away from its core. These may relate to technology, logistics, sourcing, IT systems, manufacturing, as well as cultural and organizational issues. Booz, Allen, and Hamilton conducted a study published in 2005 in which they found that firms that were in the top 10% of R&D spenders did not necessarily enjoy any better financial returns than the middle 80% of R&D spenders. The conclusion is that R&D spending does not necessarily translate into growth unless the company culture is right.[2] Organizational issues are often overlooked, yet they can be a hindrance when powerful entrenched interests would rather focus resources on core products and services rather than new products. We have seen promising new products wither on the vine inside companies because the related business

---

[1] Rita Gunther McGrath and Ian C. MacMillan, *The Entrepreneurial Mindset* (Boston: Harvard Business School Press, 2000), Chapter 8.

[2] "Mastering the Innovation Challenge Unleashing Growth and Creating Competitive Advantage," Booz / Allen / Hamilton 2005 edited by Matthew Clark.

unit—focused on making quarterly earnings per share (EPS) targets—did not want to risk commercializing a new product. Overcoming these internal competing interests is a subject unto itself, beyond the scope of this book, but there are excellent resources available.[3] The second source of uncertainty involves *External Challenges*. These may involve extending into adjacent markets with existing or new products, or entering into entirely new markets. Entering adjacent markets can present challenges because they might require new channels, new sales contacts, and even new types of customers and suppliers. Sometimes former allies become antagonists. For example, many predicted that the combination of the iPod with Motorola's RAZR cell phone into a product called the Rocker would be a recipe for success. Two immensely successful consumer products combined! Who wouldn't want this? The plan was for consumers to drop this new music phone into a cradle and load it up with songs stored on their PCs. Great idea, the only problem was that the telecom carriers wanted the consumers to download songs over their networks so that they too could make some money![4] The result was a standoff—the carriers refused to subsidize the Rocker, so its $500 cost put it outside the reach of young consumers. The outcome was a commercial failure, because the RAZR was essentially given away with each new cell phone service plan, and customers could then buy an iPod for $200. True, they had two devices in their pocket instead of one, but they saved about $300. So, you can see that making profits, even from relatively familiar new markets, is far from guaranteed.

[3] See Zenas Block and Ian C. MacMillan, *Corporate Venturing: Creating New Businesses within the Firm* (Boston: Harvard Business School Press, 1993).

[4] Roger O. Crockette, "Major Hangups over the iPod Phone," *Business Week*, March 24, 2005.

Alternatively, External Challenges are even more difficult when entering entirely new markets, where the uncertainties revolve around getting the timing right, establishing product awareness and appropriate price points, ascertaining the depth of demand, developing the right distribution channels and relationships, and perhaps (if necessary) developing a new sales force.

Building an Engineered Growth Portfolio

Combining the two sources of uncertainty stemming from Internal and External Challenges yields a simple chart that we call the Engineered Growth Portfolio chart, shown in Figure 5.1.[5]

The vertical axis of the chart measures *Internal* Challenges facing a project (which increase from bottom to top). The horizontal axis measures *External* Challenges (which increase from left to right). As we move away from the lower-left corner in any direction, uncertainty increases until it reaches its maximum in the upper-right corner of the portfolio. Using these two axes, we can begin to build a portfolio of projects and allocate resources to take advantage of projects with different timelines and purposes.

Projects in the lower-left corner of the portfolio represent enhancements to existing offerings. These core innovations extend the profitability and competitive effectiveness of current products and services; and because these projects usually address existing markets through the same channels, their valuation is based on net present value (NPV), and management's performance is assessed on delivering the numbers. We call these Core Enhancements.

---

[5] See Rita Gunther McGrath and Ian C. MacMillan, *The Entrepreneurial Mindset* (Boston: Harvard Business School Press, 2000), for further reading.

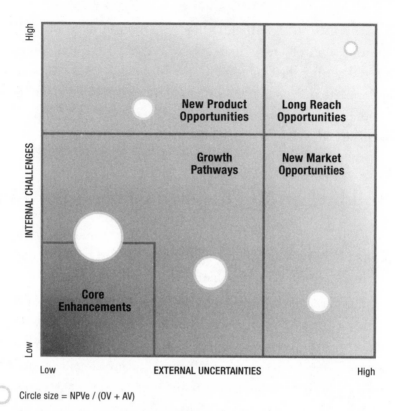

Figure 5.1   **Engineered Growth Portfolio chart**

Moving upward/outward takes us into Growth Pathways, which are innovations designed to spark next-generation profit streams. These projects are characterized by a slightly higher level of uncertainty, and valuation shifts to the use of risk-adjusted NPV. Here, managers are expected to deliver the numbers within a performance band that reflects the increased uncertainty. Projects in the growth pathways should be managed using traditional project management processes to get them into the market as quickly as possible.

The outer edge of the portfolio, running along the top and down the right side, is populated with projects that have high uncertainty associated with them, and their value comprises Engineered Value (EV) with little in the way of NPV. These projects should be considered as high-potential seeds of new offerings, and thus create call opportunities. There are three types of such opportunities in this range: New Product Opportunities (found in the upper region of the portfolio chart), New Market Opportunities (found in the area on the right), and Long Reach Opportunities (found in the upper-right corner and where the first two types of projects overlap). Long Reach Opportunities reflect an area of highly uncertain investments, with both high external and internal challenges but with inordinately high rewards if they work out. This outer edge of the portfolio (composed of New Product Opportunities, New Market Opportunities, and Long Reach Opportunities) should be evaluated as Opportunity Engineering projects where performance is assessed by the degree to which their uncertainty is being reduced and NPV being created.

We consider each of these regions within the Engineered Growth Portfolio in detail.

New Product Opportunities

Projects that face considerable Internal Challenges but low to moderate External Challenges are *New Product Opportunities.* This is when the market is ready for a new solution to an existing need, provided that the product has the right price and attributes. An example is the recently unveiled General Motors concept electric car, the Volt, which promises to deliver 40 miles per gallon wrapped up in a sleek body. The problem is that the battery technology needed to build the car at an acceptable price did not exist at the time they introduced the car in 2007. Clearly, a great-looking, high-performance car with exceptional gas mileage would face little market uncertainty if it were priced right. Unfortunately, the Volt still lacks the technology needed to be a growth pathway and needs to be treated as a new product call opportunity. We say that because of the technological challenge that the new batteries create. No one can realistically create cash flow forecasts for the car because of this uncertainty. Therefore, the only current way to value the Volt is through its Opportunity Value (OV) and Abandonment Value (AV). Therefore, we think that the Volt creates a call opportunity to develop a high-performance electric car that may (we hope) or may not (*c'est la vie*) become a huge commercial reality.

An interesting insight is that the value of new product opportunities like the Volt can often be enhanced in several ways. Acquiring needed intellectual property (IP) externally either through a license or outright purchase can speed development and thus increase the likelihood of success because the market is waiting for a solution, which in turn increases the value of the project. For instance, suppose that GM is working on the needed battery technologies for the Volt using only its own substantial internal research capabilities. But what if GM were to contract with a company that has significant IP relating to battery technology to help it produce the needed battery? Bringing in the IP from a technologically competent outsider could significantly increase the odds that the needed batteries can be produced, which makes the Volt more likely to reach the market in time to be competitive. That would have value to GM that could be calculated using Opportunity Engineering. Let's extend the example further by suggesting that GM could choose between either an exclusive or nonexclusive arrangement with the supplier of the needed battery IP. Each would presumably have a different price, and each should be considered as an opportunity with significant strategic implications for GM. Clearly, if secured by GM, the exclusive right to use the technology would have significant value because GM could block competition for some time, whereas a nonexclusive arrangement would yield lower-value first-mover advantages. Would the value of the Volt project be enhanced? Only if the joint effort yielded the battery technology needed, and therefore the maximum it should pay for the exclusive right to the IP is the difference between the Volt project as an internal effort and the potential enhanced value derived from being first to market, either with an exclusive deal or a nonexclusive deal.

New Market Opportunities

A different set of dynamics takes place when projects face considerable External Challenges. As the name implies, the source of uncertainty for *New Market Opportunities* lies largely beyond a company's control because it stems from the vagaries of the markets and the competition. These uncertainties revolve around the market size and growth rates, price points, market segments, expected market penetration rates, distribution channels, access to self space if applicable, market adjacencies, the responsiveness and character of existing/emerging competitors, product cycles, emerging trends, and so on. Essentially, new market call opportunities can be thought of as playing the role of reconnaissance in the search for the best markets. They might not generate a direct monetary return, but they will provide important intelligence about target markets. Even if they cannot tell you what to do, they can show you what *not* to do. For instance, a company that is planning to launch a new product may not be certain which market to enter first. Let's say the choice is between North America, Latin America, and Europe. Using Opportunity Engineering, each market entry strategy can be valued to determine the optimal way to launch the new product. Each of these test markets should be thought of as creating a new market call opportunity that conveys the right but not the obligation to enter that market. As such, it should be expected that some of these call opportunities will expire "worthless," meaning that they will indicate that there is no market for the new product in that region. Often, knowing what market not to enter with a new product is almost as meaningful as knowing where to go. We recognize that almost all companies do test marketing in an effort to avoid costly new product flops. By some estimates, however, 90% of new products *still* fail to generate a return on investment, so something is amiss. The benefit of Opportunity Engineering in the context of test marketing is found in its capability to value different market entry call opportunities from a menu of choices to determine the optimal strategy, and to push managers to think of market entry as a call opportunity rather than a project plan. Launching new products or entering new markets is shrouded in confusing and often contradictory signals that make for a high degree of uncertainty about what the best strategy should be. The Opportunity Engineering mindset keeps managers open to, and preferably looking for, any information that disconfirms their assumptions about the prospects for a product or market, so that they can quickly redirect their effort elsewhere before losses pile up.

New market call opportunities can take many forms. One of the most obvious is the test market, where new products are launched in a small, defined market that is a precursor to the ultimate market strategy but will nonetheless provide valuable information. Savvy companies commonly conduct test markets, but they are often not valued as call opportunities on securing a high-potential projected market.

Being able to value market tests as call opportunities serves two purposes:

1. It provides a budget number that informs how much can be spent in relation to the value of the information gained from the test, which makes it possible to select the best test market from a variety of choices.

2. The way in which test markets are conducted can be valued to find the optimal method.

Dell recently announced a departure from its established business model of selling direct to consumers by agreeing to sell its PCs in Wal-Mart stores. Dell tried this before in the early 1990s, selling through Best Buy, Costco, and Sam's Club, but found that sharing the profit margin with retailers cut too deeply into its profits.[6] However, it seems that the company's tepid revenue growth is causing it to try again.

---

[6] Matt Richtel, "Coming Soon to Wal-Mart: 2 Dell PCs," *New York Times*, May 25, 2007.

There are two ways that Dell could test the retail market. One way would be to offer its entire line of PCs in a few selected Wal-Mart stores to see which models sell the best. We would call this a vertical test, because the entire line of PCs would be tested. The second way to conduct the test, and the way chosen by Dell, is to offer only a select few models in a great many stores. This could be considered a horizontal test of the market, which allows the company to assess mass appeal. Each type of new market call opportunity provides different information.

Let's take another example from the way in which a large printing company, RR Donnelley, tested digital printing in the late 1990s. RR Donnelley's business is printing very large runs of the same document, such as magazines. Price is everything in that business. Digital printing is the exact opposite, with its promise of printing small runs on demand. Here the key to winning business is not necessarily price but speed of delivery. To be competitive, RR Donnelley would have had to build plants scattered around the country to be close to customers to meet tight delivery schedules. Rather than embark on an expensive building program, the company devised an interesting new market call opportunity. It built one plant near the Memphis, Tennessee, Federal Express hub. This gave it until the evening to get documents onto the planes for next-day delivery to its digital customers.[7] In this way, it could inexpensively test the market to determine whether its sales force could handle the different demands of the low-volume, relatively high-price digital printing market without risking a great deal of money. If you think about this new market call opportunity and consider how to create maximum call opportunity value, would you build a plant in Memphis or rent a plant? What if you did not have any plant at all, but rather outsourced the printing to a local digital printer to see whether the RR Donnelley sales force could be effective with smaller

---

[7] David A. Garvin and Artemis March, "R. R. Donnelley & Sons: The Digital Division," Harvard Business School Case, January 12, 1996.

clients? If you assume equivalent revenue from all three ways of implementing the business, the optimal value would stem from the lowest fixed-cost structure. So, the greatest call opportunity value in this example would come from having RR Donnelley outsource the actual printing to a third party until it was sure that it wanted to enter the market for digital printing, even though it would earn a smaller net margin (or even lose money) on this business. This is because production costs would be exactly tied to sales, so except for the sales force, all the costs would be variable—no business, no cost. Now that's the Opportunity Engineering mindset!

Long-Reach Opportunities

Where the New Market and New Product Opportunities overlap in the upper-right corner of the portfolio, we find projects that have high external and internal uncertainties associated with them. Although they face long odds, these projects *must* hold the possibility of generating breakthrough products in the future.

An example at the writing of this book is news that researchers have developed a memory chip about the size of a white blood cell that is capable of holding 160,000 bits of data. This project has tremendous uncertainty surrounding both the internal technical issues and the external market issues that have to be overcome before it can lead to new products. The potential for this technology is enormous, but the development cycle will be long and uncertain.

When companies that have the resources invest in Long Reach Opportunities, they should be managed with the explicit intention of reducing uncertainty. When these sorts of projects do begin to show some degree of promise, their uncertainty will come down, and the project will shift to become either a New Market Opportunity to resolve remaining external uncertainties or a New Product Opportunity to reduce lingering internal uncertainties.

Long Reach opportunities do not necessarily require companies to tackle major technical and market challenges. They can be based on products or services that are well established in other firms but represent a radical departure from your company's normal business.

Take, for instance, Honda's entry into the general aviation market through its new division, Honda Aviation. In late 2006, Honda began taking orders for its new business jet with a price in the $3 million range. Business jets have obviously been a big business for a long time for many companies, but for Honda it must have been considered a Long Reach Opportunity. It was certainly unconventional for a leading auto manufacturer to be entering the aircraft industry. (SAAB, being the only major exception, began with military jets and then backed into automobiles.) In the beginning of the project, Honda faced high levels of external and internal uncertainties. Internal issues would have ranged from technology questions, concerning how to build an airframe, to producing composite materials and gaining certifications for the aircraft from unfamiliar regulatory bodies worldwide. It's interesting that Honda chose to mitigate one of its greatest challenges, designing and manufacturing the engines, by partnering with GE aircraft, the respected leader in commercial aviation engines. Heretofore, Honda has always used its core competence of small engine manufacturing as a unifying theme in its product extensions. External uncertainties included the capability of an automobile and motorbike manufacturer to carry its brand into entirely new markets that required entirely new distribution and sales channels. Clearly, everyone respects Honda's engineering and manufacturing ability when it comes to cars, but would people buy an aircraft from Honda? The answer is more likely to be yes with the GE aircraft engine connection, which stripped away many major technical and marketing uncertainties from the project.

In the service sector, UPS provides a good example of a Long Reach Opportunity with its service alliance with Toshiba. Previously, when customers called Toshiba with a service need on their laptop, they sent it off to a Toshiba service center, where it was repaired and then returned in a few days. Now customers have their laptops picked up by UPS and repaired in a UPS facility by UPS employees who were trained by Toshiba. The turnaround time has been reduced to three days as a result. Although UPS must have had many of the skills in house before Toshiba approached them, this was still a long-reach opportunity because it opened up other related opportunities to provide remote services for client companies.

In closing the discussion of product, market, and long-reach portfolio opportunities, we want to stress that they should not remain so for long! If you are not reducing uncertainties as you work your way from CheckPoint to CheckPoint in your DDP, think seriously of shutting down the project and deploying your talent to projects that do reduce uncertainty.

Growth Pathways

When new market and new product call opportunities mature to the point that they show commercial promise, they move down the portfolio closer to the lower-left side into the region that we call Growth Pathways. These form the basis for new products that will propel your company's growth in the near future. When projects become Growth Pathways, the External and Internal Challenges should have been largely reduced. The product has been developed and prototyped, test marketing should have been completed, and managers should have fairly reliable data on the size of the applicable market segments on which to base sales estimates. The distribution channels should be identified and reasonably well understood, and organizational issues have been resolved. One key remaining source of uncertainty often concerns competitive reaction. If the product is not entirely new, managers should have made assumptions regarding which competitors will be the most likely to retaliate, when they will do so, and how they will chose to compete.

When projects become Growth Pathways, two things should happen. One is that their OV will have been largely eroded because uncertainty surrounding the new offering has been deliberately reduced. This is the result of replacing many of the assumptions with knowledge, or at least having narrowed the confidence interval surrounding the remaining assumption values as the development effort proceeds. As uncertainty declines, it is replaced by the risk of execution against the plan. Think of uncertainty as being nebulous, whereas risk can be measured. In the beginning, when projects represent opportunities, it is impossible to assign probabilities to the outcome of the development effort, because there is simply too much uncertainty. If they succeed to represent new product pathways, it is possible to begin thinking in terms of the probability of success. When projects move to become Growth Pathways, there is a shift from OV, in the outer regions of the portfolio where uncertainty is high, to risk-adjusted NPV. As OV erodes, it is replaced by a shift toward NPV, which is what you want to see.

We see here the practical application of our contention that project investments can be engineered to include both OV and NPV to guide decision making. Said differently, project value should be considered as comprising a risk component (NPVe) and an uncertainty component (OV). Remember that OV is nice to have, but you need NPV to make payroll. Besides shifting sources of valuation when projects move from the Opportunity region of the portfolio to the Growth Pathways region, the way the project must be managed shifts, too. Reduced uncertainty means that management shifts from Opportunity Engineering, with its emphasis on testing assumptions, to traditional project management, with emphasis on making numbers and meeting deadlines. The reason is simple: When projects move to the Pathways phase of development, they are no longer call opportunities; they are now offerings, and need to get into the market quickly.

Core Enhancements

The lower-left corner of the portfolio represents projects we call *Core Enhancements*. These projects represent well-understood improvements to existing products and services. They are vitally important to every company because they are essential to maintaining competitiveness, delivering cash flow, and meeting financial expectations of the market. Core Enhancements are improvements to existing products that are intended to increase or at least maintain the product's appeal. They are low-risk development efforts because they usually rely on known distribution and sales channels and well-known markets. In addition, production and logistics are similar to what already is done. Because these projects entail low uncertainty, their value is based on traditional NPV. These core projects are managed using traditional processes that stress speed, efficiency, and quality.

There is a cautionary tale here, and that is that Core Enhancements are usually insufficient to maintain consistent growth. This is especially the case in volatile, competitive industries. Let's consider Motorola's hugely successful Razr cell phone. The company has brought successive versions of the Razr to market, the latest of which is the Razr V3, with enhanced operating features and racy colors. Motorola sold a total of 75 million Razrs in the two years following its introduction in the fourth quarter of 2004—a huge success. But Motorola's focus on core enhancements concerning the Razr kept it from focusing on subsequent innovations that would be needed to keep up with its competitors that were focused on the next generation of phones that moved the industry toward a convergence of the cell phone with the PC, as well as with music and game players. Without competing products, Motorola was left defenseless, and it could resort only to continual price cuts until the profit margin on the Razr fell from 11.9% in the third quarter 2006 to 4.4% in the fourth quarter of 2007. This resulted in a crushing 48% decline in the company's fourth quarter 2006 net income.[8] The Razr, once a high-tech marvel, had fallen to commodity status within two years of its introduction. This example illustrates what happens when companies fail to push resources out into the opportunity regions of the portfolio to create a balanced development strategy.

Compare this to the path chosen by Apple. The iPod restored the company just as the Razr restored Motorola. The difference is that Apple used the cash flow from core enhancements to the iPod (like the Nano) to fund call opportunities on its next-generation consumer product, the recently introduced iPhone. Only a continual stream of projects from the opportunity regions of the portfolio will keep your company on a growth path. If Apple is unable to sustain the stream of new projects, it, too, will end up in trouble.

We think of the projects in the Portfolio as forming a metaphorical cascade of opportunities for your company. We illustrate this in Figure 5.2. They can begin as Long Reach Opportunities (shown at the upper left), which can have negative NPV but a lot of OV. Projects can also start as New Market or New Product Opportunities, in which case they may have some positive NPV along with substantial OV. Long Reach Opportunities that show promise will then flow down to become either New Product Opportunities or New Market Opportunities, depending on the major source of uncertainty concerning their development. Those that fail to meet expectations at CheckPoints during the development process are eliminated. As a result, the number of projects in the opportunities area of the portfolio should usually be larger than the number of Growth Pathways.

---

[8] Cheng, Roger and Yuan, Li, "Motorola's Strategy to Get an Overhaul", *The Wall Street Journal*, January 20, 2007.

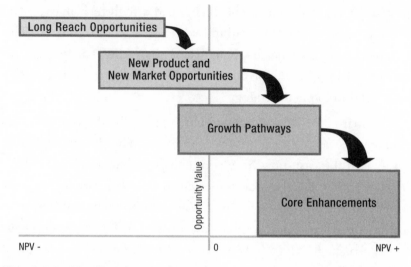

Figure 5.2   The Opportunity Cascade

How to Use the Engineered Growth Portfolio

The Engineered Growth Portfolio is intended to be an aid in your strategic planning process. For instance, a company could use the Portfolio to allocate resources on the corporate level, between the various types of categories. Then, each business would reallocate resources across the Portfolio in accordance with their individual strategic mission. For instance, core businesses tend to emphasize generating earnings and cash flow, so their focus is on doing things faster, better, and cheaper. As a result, their investments would be predominantly Core Enhancements and limited Growth Pathways. For business units that are in rapid growth markets that offer higher returns than core businesses, it might be appropriate to invest more heavily in the opportunity regions of the portfolio.

In Figure 5.3, we have added numbers along the horizontal and vertical axes of the engineered growth portfolio. These numbers allow projects to be positioned on the portfolio in accordance with the level of uncertainty inherent to their development. The numbers shown are generic suggestions, and they should be tailored to your firm to reflect your specific situation and your firm's tolerance for uncertainty and risk. We provide some initial guidelines (derived from McGrath and MacMillan, *The Entrepreneurial Mindset,* Harvard University Press, 2000) for doing this in the appendix attached to this chapter, but encourage you to develop your own firm-specific scales by deleting questions in the appendix that are not relevant to your firm and adding scoring questions that are relevant. The numbers increase along the horizontal and vertical axes to reflect increased uncertainty about each project, and they relate to how each project scores on the brief questionnaires below that tap the level of uncertainty surrounding projects. These questionnaires are discussed in detail later, so for the moment accept that there is a systematic way to position your projects on the Engineered Growth Portfolio.

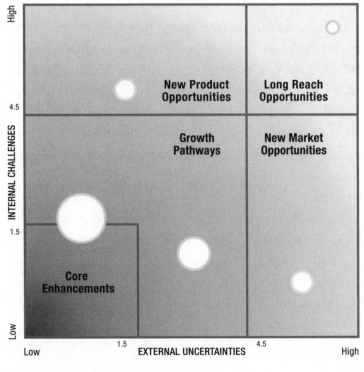

Circle size = NPVe / (OV + AV)

Figure 5.3 Engineered Growth Portfolio chart

We depict each project as a circle, with its size based on the ratio of the elements comprising the structured value of the project. In other words, the size of the circle depicting each project is based on the relation circle size = (NPVe) / OV + AV. Thus, the size of a circle is the ratio of a project's NPVe to its Opportunity and Abandonment values, a measure of the "density ratio" of the opportunity, the beef-to-smoke ratio—how much NPV beef there is to the much more tenuous value derived from OV and AV. If the NPVe is negative, which can happen for a highly uncertain project, the circle is gray shaded rather than white. In the early stages of a project when its NPVe will usually be small due to high uncertainty and its OV and AV large, dividing the small NPVe by the large OV and AV will result in a small number, hence a small circle. Therefore, a larger circle is better than a smaller one. This provides a useful graphic depiction of where resources are being directed.

As we said, a larger circle means that the NPV exceeds the OV of a project, which in our view is generally a good thing. It means that there is a great deal of confidence surrounding the project, which is what we expect to see if projects are in the Growth Pathways area of the portfolio. Projects in the outer opportunities region of the portfolio would not normally have this type of surety surrounding them, so pictorially their circle sizes would be smaller than Growth Pathways projects and certainly smaller than Core Enhancements. This provides a quick visual reference for managers because as money is spent on projects, their circle size should be increasing as more is learned. If that is not happening, continued spending on the project should be called into question—the project should be redirected or shut down and resources redeployed to projects where learning is taking place. Similarly, projects should move toward the lower-left side of the portfolio as more is learned. If a project has no NPV, depict it with a dot to indicate its existence and position within the Engineered Growth Portfolio.

The final piece of our Engineered Growth Portfolio plot is to enter a number in each circle to represent the EV of the project. Figure 5.4 depicts an Engineered Growth Portfolio plot with several projects, specifically projects marked A, B, C, and D.

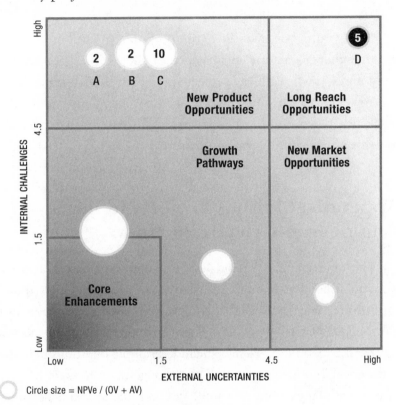

Figure 5.4   Engineered Growth Portfolio chart

Look at projects A, B, and C, and assume they are *very* close together. Comparing projects A and B, we see that both have an EV of 2, but B has a larger circle size, which means there is "more beef and less smoke" to project B, making project B preferred over A. Now look at project C compared to B. They both have the same circle size, but C has a higher EV of 10, which means C takes priority over B. So, the mapping of individual projects enables you to make judgments as to which projects should be prioritized. Now look at project D, which is gray, indicating negative NPVe. The number 5 suggests that EV is largely due to the OV and AV components massively compensating for the negative NPVe. This has all the qualities of a long-reach opportunity and needs to be managed ruthlessly to reduce the cost of failure and reduce uncertainty fast.

Finally, after you map the entire portfolio, you will be able to ask whether there is a sufficient balance of short-term Core Enhancement and Growth Pathway projects to deliver short-term cash flows and revenue growth, and whether you have enough new product and new market opportunities and perhaps some long-reach opportunities to deliver longer-term growth platforms.

Appendix: Plotting Projects in the Engineered Growth Portfolio

The questionnaires found in this section are based on original work published by McGrath and MacMillan[9] in an attempt to quantify the Internal and External Challenges that surround projects in the Engineered Growth Portfolio. There is one questionnaire for each source of uncertainty. We have included sample questions to help get you started, but we suggest that you change them to meet the needs of your company or business unit. We find that as teams become familiar with the process, they realize that some of the questions really do not pertain, and they readily come up with better ones. Because each question has the same weight in the scoring process, substituting your own will not change how projects are plotted on the portfolio. If your team thinks that there are too many questions to be answered, eliminate some of them. Because the resulting score is an average, it does not matter how many questions there are. The one caveat is that

---

[9]   Excerpted by permission of Harvard Business School Press from *The Entrepreneurial Mindset*, by R. G. McGrath and Ian MacMillan, pages 174–175, copyright © 2000 by the Harvard Business School Publishing Corporation; all rights reserved.

the questionnaires should be consistent across projects so that you have a uniform way of deciding how projects should be evaluated.

The questionnaire should be filled out by the team that will be working on the project, enhanced by people with functional insights (marketing, sales, operations, legal, and so on) plus anyone with expertise in the industry that will be entered. Results of the process should be reported as an average score for each question, together with their maximum and minimum scores to facilitate an analysis of projects under consideration. Because they rely on subjective estimates, the results cannot provide a perfect correlation to the true uncertainty surrounding each project, but the process is nonetheless useful. First, it provides a uniform and somewhat quantitative way to look at where your company's growth projects are deployed. We find that the discussion of whether or not projects are properly represented on the portfolio is extremely useful in and of itself. Second, it often highlights that many companies are simply too conservative, even though they might think quite the opposite to be true.

We find in practice that most projects within companies are clustered in the lower-left quadrant of the portfolio, representing Core Enhancements. This clustering indicates insufficient investment in new areas to continue to propel growth. Perhaps of greater consequence is the realization that an overly conservative investment approach opens a company to a disruptive competitive attack. If this is the case, the next step is to decide on the level of resources that are to be committed to each of the five investment types. This forces managers to push beyond their comfort zone looking for new ideas with which to populate the outer regions of the portfolio. Given the choice, managers are unlikely to fund an uncertain project if they can instead increase advertising spending for existing products. However, if managers are required to find new opportunities, they will do so, especially if they can use Opportunity Engineering to create a safe harbor. A corollary portfolio requirement is that money allocated to New Product Opportunities cannot instead be used to fund a Growth Pathway or Core Enhancement (everyone's favorite). When projects are competing for resources only with similar projects (such as other product opportunities) and not competing with dissimilar projects (such as Core Enhancements), the effect is to force the selection of the best projects within each category.

Using the questionnaires to position projects on the portfolio also identifies the key areas of uncertainty surrounding new projects.

Internal Challenges

Next to each question, answer with a score that ranges from 1 to 5, with 1 indicating a low level of uncertainty and 5 indicating a very high level of uncertainty.	**Score**
1. Identification of the key uncertainties facing the project	
2. Time needed to complete development	
3. Budget estimates for development costs	
4. Needed IP can be developed or acquired	
5. Availability of capital to fund development	
6. Internal project champion has been identified	
7. Degree of project fit with current corporate strategy	
8. Business unit interest in project	
9. Availability of needed skills	
10. Development team's cohesion around the project	
11. Availability of production capacity	
12. Danger of cannibalization of existing products	
13. Logistics needs	
14. Project abandonment value	
Total score divided by 14 to get average score	

Broadly, if a project happens to be classified as a New Market Opportunity, the Opportunity Engineering process should front load the project with CheckPoints that can test the market-based assumptions. After the market assumptions have been favorably resolved, the project may either become a Growth Pathway or it might shift to become a New Product Opportunity to resolve the internal uncertainties.

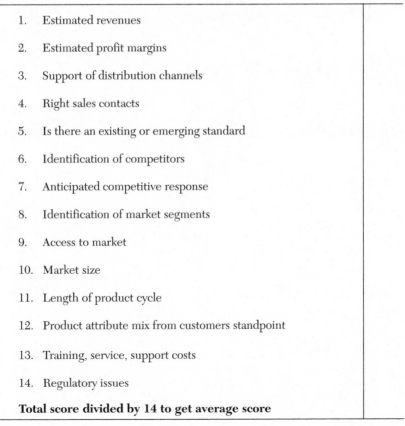

External Challenges

Next to each question, answer with a score that ranges from 1 to 5, with 1 indicating a low level of uncertainty and 5 indicating a very high level of uncertainty.	**Score**
1. Estimated revenues	
2. Estimated profit margins	
3. Support of distribution channels	
4. Right sales contacts	
5. Is there an existing or emerging standard	
6. Identification of competitors	
7. Anticipated competitive response	
8. Identification of market segments	
9. Access to market	
10. Market size	
11. Length of product cycle	
12. Product attribute mix from customers standpoint	
13. Training, service, support costs	
14. Regulatory issues	
Total score divided by 14 to get average score	

6

Applying Opportunity Engineering Throughout Your Business

Opportunity Engineering applies to your business wherever and whenever uncertainty exists about future outcomes. In this chapter, we explore some major areas in which OE can prove helpful in running your business.

Joint Ventures, Licenses, and Alliances

Coalition activities such as joint ventures, licenses, and alliances can meaningfully reduce the uncertainty surrounding a strategy. For instance, a joint venture can mitigate your market uncertainties when your partner company has distribution channels or contacts that will allow faster market access for a new product. This affects uncertainty by reducing the time to market and reducing costs. Licenses from your partner can provide faster access to a needed technology and thus reduce the cost, time, and uncertainty of developing the capability in house, which can reduce time to market. Alliances serve much the same purpose, in that they are formed to reduce costs, save time, or gain access to new markets and capabilities more cheaply and more quickly than would be possible working alone.

Let's consider an example of how the concept of Engineered Value (EV) can pay off by guiding managers to make better decisions when they are entering into joint ventures. As an example, we worked with a well-run conservative industrial company, which we will call CoreCo, that was thinking of entering into a joint venture that would provide entree into a politically unstable country that nonetheless offered tremendous upside market opportunities. CoreCo's weighted average cost of capital was 9%, but because of perceived political risk in the target country, the CFO insisted that the management team add a 9% risk premium to the cost of capital, for a total discount rate of 18%. Nearly everyone was enthusiastic about the deal, but they were disappointed when the standard financial analysis that showed a net present value (NPV) of minus $80,000. This suggested that the deal would destroy shareholder value and thus should be rejected, although the numbers were a close call. This defied their intuition that it was a good investment because it opened up manifold other opportunities in the region. Using the EVS software, we used a decision-tree approach to value the investment. Again, the numbers are simplified for ease of exposition; the actual analysis was considerably more complex.

Management developed three potential return profiles from the joint venture (JV): good, moderate, or bad. Within each outcome, they estimated the following sets of returns:

> JV investment = $17 million to $22 million, with the most likely being $20 million (The negotiations were just under way.)

The present value of the returns resulting from the JV were expected to be within the following ranges:

- If the *good* outcome occurred (given an estimated 80% probability), the current value of the JV would be between $12 and $32 million, with the most likely return of $30 million.
- The *moderate* outcome (given a 15% probability) would have an expected current value of between $3 and $15 million, with $10 million the most likely.
- The *bad* outcome (given a 5% probability of a national uprising) had a current value between $500,000 and $5 million, with $2 million the most likely.

Therefore, the company could invest an expected $20 million, with a worst-case discounted return of between $500,000 (a 5% probability, but it could well occur) and a best-case return of $30 million (with an 80% probability). This is an enormous spread, so the NPV came out to be slightly negative. Common sense would suggest the heck with the numbers and make the investment because it makes gut-feel sense. However, this is tantamount to abandoning all discipline and opening the floodgates for all sorts of wild-eyed investments.

Using the EVS software, based on the above distributions, the value of the JV was as follows:

$$EV = NPVe + OV + AV$$
NPVe = -$80,000
OV = $610,000
AV = $0
EV = $530,000

This supported management's intuition that the deal should be done. What OE did was to capture the potential value of the asymmetric return in this investment. The problem of going with gut feel is that it becomes much more complex when you are looking at two such uncertain investments. Then intuition begins to fail because the decision is not just about going ahead with one deal, but the choice between deals. Whose gut feel is "gutsier?" Unless you have some way to rank the potential outcomes of each investment, knowing which one is better becomes sheer guesswork or sheer politics. Make it three potential investments and you might as well throw darts.

On the other hand, OE provides estimates of the potential upside and downside of each project based on the EV to guide selection to the best investment of the three.

Ramping Up the Complexity

A wrinkle with the CoreCo example, which made it more compli-
cated, was that in addition to investing in the basic JV, a potential second round of investment was possible. The original JV was directed
toward bulk customers; if the basic plant worked out, however, a second-stage plant could be built that might allow the firm to deliver
higher-quality product to serve high-end customers at higher prices.
If the first-stage plant proved successful, the second stage would require an additional investment of $3 million in year 3. These extra
sales were clearly more speculative, but in the context of OE they
should be counted toward value. Schematically, this second investment changed the potential outcomes, as shown in Figure 6.1.

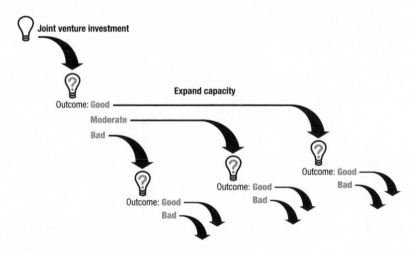

Figure 6.1   CoreCo joint venture outcomes

Management thought that this further-downstream investment
could result in the following three outcomes:

1. If the results of the *original* JV were *good,* the second stage from expansion could generate two outcomes:

   Good outcome for second stage—80% probability of between $3 and $8 million, with $6 million the most likely value, which was expected to occur in year 3

   Bad outcome for second stage—20% probability of between $1 and $4 million value, with the most likely value of $3 million in year 4

2. Following the same thought process, but beginning from a *moderate* original JV outcome:

   Good outcome for second stage—70% probability of between $2 to $5 million value, with $4 million most likely in the year 4

   Bad outcome for second stage—30% probability of between $1 to $2 million, with $1.5 million considered most likely

3. Beginning from the *bad* original JV outcome, they still expected to continue with expanded capacity, but with diminished hopes of success, resulting in these outcome probabilities:

   Good outcome for second stage—40% probability of between $1 to $2 million, with $1.5 million considered most likely

   Bad outcome for second stage—60% probability of between $500,000 to $1 million, with $700,000 million considered most likely

Finally, by doing some OE, the project team came up with a possible abandonment value (AV), which arose from management's estimate that the second-stage capacity could be sold to another company for $1 million (again these numbers are disguised) should the firm decide to stop production for high-end users. This is why the concept of creating AV is so important for engineered investments. It drives managers to find creative ways to mitigate the downside of uncertain investments, whether they are JVs, acquisitions, or new product launches.

When we took this second stage of the JV into account, the numbers changed in the following way:

EV = NPVe + OV + AV
NPVe = $560,000
OV = $380,000
AV = $140,000
EV = $1,070,000

The EV almost doubled because we were able to value the call on the second stage of the JV, and also engineer AV. The EVS software provided a way to value the positive uncertainty underlying the business.

Scenario Planning

Many firms engage in scenario planning to assess the impact of uncertain external events on their businesses. Scenario planning develops several different views of the future, which usually pertain to the uncertainties about combinations of external contingencies involving products, services, technologies, supply systems, regulations, and competitive forces. Although scenarios and their insights are important to know in and of themselves, they do not always suggest concrete actions to mitigate the impact of negative scenarios as they emerge. The difficulty lies in separating signal from noise. By the time signals point to which scenario is emerging, it is often too late to do much about it. OE can be used to design low-cost CheckPoints that provide signals as to which scenarios are emerging.

Designing such CheckPoints is always a challenge, but the idea is to think about which early indicators would signal which scenario is emerging. For instance, if a scenario relating to a new product development effort is that a recession could occur that would disrupt market entry, it would do no good to wait for the U.S. Commerce Department to tally up the sales information from around the country and report the latest GDP growth rate to devise an effective hedge. It would be too late. Once the signal is strong, its value is lost because there are no degrees of freedom left. Instead, think about what interacts with the economy that can create recessions to gain an early insight into the emerging future. It is generally accepted that recessions can be caused by higher oil prices, so instead of tracking economic activity, track the price trends in crude oil to gain an early insight into the probability that a recession scenario is occurring. In part, the power of OE comes into play because it motivates managers to design preplanned responses to emerging information, because that creates OV or AV. In the context of the growth portfolio, the response would be to create New Market Opportunities or New Product Opportunities that could serve to hedge against the impact of higher oil prices, or some other course of action. The Chevy Volt that we discussed in Chapter 5, "Creating an Engineered Growth Portfolio," as a New Product Opportunity serves as a hedge for GM that will attain maximum value if oil prices increase, because it should mitigate the impact on the company's core vehicle sales.

In general, the problem illustrated in Figure 6.2 is that the ability to use the knowledge about which future is emerging decays as the signal strength increases. The vertical axis plots the signal strength that a scenario is emerging; think of it as the probability of occurrence. The horizontal axis measures time as it marches toward the right, where, finally, the future can be known for certain. If we look at the upward sloping line labeled Emerging Signal Strength, it climbs progressively as time goes from some early point, labeled t − x on the horizontal axis toward t − 1, which is when the future has emerged. At the same time, the downward sloping line is measuring the degrees of freedom you have to act, where the fewer degrees of freedom you have is interpreted as having little ability to change course. When the iceberg is 20 miles away, you have many ways (degrees of freedom) to change course; when the iceberg is off the port bow, you have no degrees of freedom. Returning to Figure 6.2, at time = t − x, the Emerging Signal Strength line is low (the iceberg is far away and barely discernable), but the Degrees of Freedom line is high, meaning that there are many ways to avoid the emerging iceberg. At time = t − 3, there is more information about the iceberg and its location, but our ability to change course is somewhat more limited, which is shown by the decline in the Degrees of Freedom line. If we wait until the iceberg is in plain sight, the Degrees of Freedom line has dropped to its lowest point because there is nothing that we can do to avoid the collision.

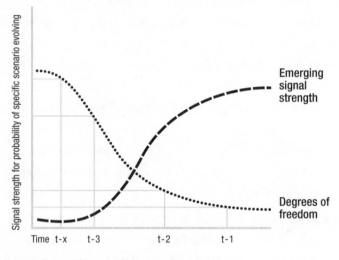

Figure 6.2   Information quality versus usefulness

The thought process behind Figure 6.2 is not new (it was defined by a Rand Corporation study for the U.S. military some time ago), but the way to use it with emerging opportunities is. If we combine the insight that our ability to profit from emerging trends is directly related to how early we can detect a trend, projects can be designed to create CheckPoint signals as to whether that trend is emerging. For example, suppose that we were working on a project that is highly sensitive to the price of oil. Let's look at a highly simplified example to illustrate the thinking process. Again, much more complex situations can be handled with this thinking process, but we stick with a simple example for the sake of expediency. So, keeping it simple, suppose the big scenario concern is that there could be a disruption in the supply of oil from the Middle East. What kind of CheckPoint indicators could the firm put in place that would signal an increasing probability this disruption would take place? First, set up some precursor events that are likely to occur before this takes place and then build indicators that these events are emerging. One such t – 1 event would be the collapse of the House of Saud. So, we could put in place indicators of political radicalization in Saudi Arabia, which in turn would be indicated by a t – 2 precursor indicator: increasing internal political unrest in that country. If these indicators go on an uptick, it would behoove the firm to look at other indicators of possible oil supply disruption in the Middle East. A second major t – 1 indicator would be a major al Qaeda success in other Middle East countries such as Syria, Afghanistan, or Pakistan, whose precursor t – 2 indicators would be increasing local support for al Qaeda activities in those countries. A third major t – 1 indicator would be direct interference by Iran in Iraq, with the corresponding t – 2 indicators being increasing militancy of Iran. (Any readers getting nervous about oil supply prospects?) If several of these indicators tick up, the firm would be well advised to configure a strategy around the increasingly likely emergence of this scenario, using OE principles to create opportunity puts and abandonments for the event that this does occur.

Mergers and Acquisitions

With the odds of success from M&A activity running at about 40% (using value creation for the acquirer's shareholders as the metric), it is difficult to think of an acquisition as anything but having purchased an option on some "uncertain but hoped-for high-potential" outcome. We suspect that the overused (and often misused) term *synergy* is really an intuitive way of saying that there is potentially more value to an acquisition than may be apparent from the NPV calculation. Sometimes it is difficult to think about how to create EV in a merger context, because after the deal closes, there is little choice but to go forward. This is typical binary thinking that considers only success and failure as outcomes. However, there are ways to create additional value ahead of the merger if we consider the sources of uncertainty and how we might mitigate them. We find that just the thought process involved in finding alternatives to binary outcomes can prove effective in creating deal terms that are more beneficial to both parties. An obvious example is the common practice of structuring an acquisition with earn-out provisions. This leads to a variable purchase price because the final total price paid is determined in part by the success of the acquisition in creating stockholder value. Often, earn-out provisions that satisfy the needs of the buyer are offset by a higher purchase price to satisfy the needs of the seller. The value of earn-out provisions is readily computed using the EVS software.

EV is also created when the acquirer has "the right" but not the obligation to invest more money to expand the acquired business if it is proving to be successful. Therefore, the initial purchase creates a call on further expansion of the target company's business. Why not understand what this option to expand is worth before settling on a price for the target?

Yet another source of EV that is usually overlooked is the possible AV of an acquisition. If the acquisition is not proving to be the success envisioned, it can be sold. Having the option to abandon creates value because the acquirer has the right but not the obligation to abandon the investment for a range of prices that could be estimated at the very beginning of the acquisition. Simply thinking about how to create AV in an acquisition can bring valuable insights into the way the acquisition is selected, priced, and negotiated, as well as how it is managed after the closing.

Let's use the acquisition of Household International (HI) by HSBC (Hong Kong Shanghai Bank) to illustrate how to think about creating EV in acquisitions. HSBC specializes in wealth management with a global brand. HI, in contrast, specializes in making small loans to credit-impaired consumers. The stark contrast was evident to all concerned. Wall Street hammered HSBC's stock price after the merger. The bank paid $14 billion for HI, roughly ten times its earnings. Investors could not see a link between the two companies, and especially at that price, the NPV of the deal was not particularly attractive in light of the perceived strategic mismatch. If we use a (low) 10% discount rate and hold the $1.4 billion HI profit constant over a 10-year period, the NPV of the investment would be approximately *negative* $5.4 billion. (We calculated this without considering any annuity value to the investment after year 10—a simplifying assumption.) Clearly, there was the anticipation on the part of HSBC of substantial new business opportunities in the future.

Indeed, investors and analysts did not see what HSBC could bring to the deal beyond its balance sheet, which would reduce the cost of borrowing for HI but do little else. No one really saw what HI brought to HSBC because the bank was not in the same markets, and it was feared that the merger would diminish the Bank's brand. Beyond the obvious, the two companies differed even further in how they did business. HSBC, according to the bank's CEO John Bond,[1] used only five data points in evaluating a mortgage loan before making a decision. In contrast, HI used extremely sophisticated proprietary psycho-demographic statistical programs to evaluate 200 behavioral data points for each applicant in evaluating a loan request. The company used this program to preset credit limits for every U.S. citizen, all of whom were constantly solicited via direct mail. How different could these two companies be in both market segments and culture? An analyst report dated December 2002, regarding the merger from SchroderSalomonSmith-Barney typifies the negative view of the merger. Among many concerns raised by various analysts were the following:

1. HI will make HSBC much more credit sensitive, driving it from having the lowest exposure to bad debts of any European bank to one of the highest. This will make HSBC earnings much more volatile. Including HI bad debts will consume 55% of HSBC earnings as opposed to its premerger 16% exposure to bad debts.

---

[1] Harvard Business School Publishing case interview: "HSBC: The Household Acquisition," 2006.

2. The volatility of HI bad debt write-offs will be the equivalent of HSBC earnings in 2003, less those made in Asia (excluding Hong Kong), North America, and South America.

3. From the period from 2000 to 2003, HSBC increased its consumer loan exposure in the United States by 4% due to its concern about debt levels. At the same time, HI increased its book of consumer loans by 50% to $107 billion. This flies in the face of HSBC's cautious approach to lending for which it was held in high regard by investors.

These financial concerns say nothing about the difficulties to be encountered while merging systems and cultures. So, it was expected that investors would bid down the HSBC price earnings ratio, degrading its stock price.

But is this the only way to look at the acquisition? How might we slice out the risk of the acquisition while building and going for a large upside reward? This is what senior management was thinking—although more intuitively than in EV terms.

The senior management of HSBC had a different vision. John Bond, then HSBC CEO, was not buying HI for its American business, which was at the heart of the analysts' objections. What Sir Bond saw in the acquisition was the potential to bring the HI consumer lending expertise to the nascent Asian consumer credit markets, such as in China and India. Consider the potential of issuing one billion HSBC credit cards with just a $200 credit limit. That would be $200 billion of credit, with resulting new net revenues potentially in the $10 billion range, depending on interest rate spreads.

A problem is that there was not, and still is not, any consumer data in the developing economies of Central Europe and Asia of the sort used by HI in the United States. Credit scoring does not exist in the emerging markets, and there is little, if any, information on repayment patterns. But what if this data could be obtained? How much would it be worth to own the most sophisticated issuer of consumer debt when that consumer data does become available in the emerging markets? Of course, many uncertainties surround this vision. It will be years before the consumer data of the sort used by HI can be collected (although that is already beginning to be done in Hungary), and who knows whether these new consumers in Asia and Central Europe will gravitate to Western-style consumer debt? Other issues pertain to the applicability of the HI analytical model to other markets, such as the following:

- Applicability of the deep HI understanding of U.S. consumer behavior patterns to consumers in Asia and other regions
- Consumer interest in debt financing in emerging markets
- Regulatory response to credit card issuance and interest rates
- Cultural fit between the two companies and their managers

These questions are very consequential in that they can have a deep impact on the outcome of the acquisition.

Let's consider how OE might change the way this acquisition was viewed. The EV of the acquisition of HI would have the now familiar elements of $EV = NPVe + OV + AV$. The question is how to create the various elements of value to separate risk from reward.

Using our familiar OE catechism, we could ask first, how might it be possible to engineer the NPV in a situation such as this? The concerns about the acquisition revolved mostly around the hidden risks in the HI portfolio. These are as follows:

1. Given its rapid growth, the uncertainty concerning the overheated U.S. debt market in 2002
2. The reliability of HI customer segments many considered to be dicey

Let's look at how using OE thinking can impact the value of the proposed merger.

Engineering Opportunity 1: Two-stage purchase: The value of HI might be substantially higher or lower than the $14 billion, due to the volatility of its loss provisions. This cannot be captured in traditional discounted cash flow analysis. Trying to capture volatility with discounted cash flow to arrive at a net present value engineered (NPVe) would require reliable cash flow estimates and probabilities of each possible outcome of the lending environment for HI, both good and bad, as if that were possible! However, it can be a part of the EV of a deal such as this, and it should be considered. EV is based on equal probabilities for all the values of the HI portfolio, but it takes into account only the positive outcomes for valuation. If we create a staged purchase structure, with a fixed purchase price, we have an asymmetric return because the HSBC would not have to close on the full equity of the target company. Therefore, the negative outcomes of the HI volatility do not have to be accounted for because HSBC would not be exposed to them.

So, one way to engineer the NPV would be to structure the acquisition as a staged purchase that would limit the downside risk to HSBC if investors' concerns proved to be warranted. The bank would acquire a minority interest at first so that it would have less at risk in the worst case. Doing so would limit the chance of a large loss. If sellers are amenable to this sort of staged purchase, the usual tradeoff is a higher ultimate price to be paid for the acquisition. The size of this premium is based on the time value of money, meaning that the buyer has to compensate the seller for lost interest and the opportunity cost incurred by not having all the sales proceeds in hand at the initial closing. The trouble is, often the final premium depends less on the true value and more on the negotiating skills of the parties to the transaction, because there is lack of clarity on the true value of the staged purchase given a volatile acquisition target.

Where OE can really help is in calculating the correct value of the delayed payment. The EV calculation of an acquisition provides insight into what staging a purchase price is worth, which sets the ceiling for negotiations. For example, suppose HSBC offered to pay

$3 billion for 30% of the equity of HI, and had the right but not the obligation to buy the rest for $12 billion in three years. The total price would be $15 billion, giving a $1 billion premium for the delay on the original price offered. Using the EVS software for this two-stage case, the EV of the acquisition would be as follows:

NPVe = –$6.16 billion

OV = $5.76 billion

AV = $740 million

EV = $340 million

In this simple example, the effect of staging an acquisition has on a deal is apparent. Also, the benefit of being able to value the staging is apparent—it sets the upper limit on any premium demanded by HI stockholders for allowing HSBC to delay purchasing, namely the formal $1 billion premium of the offer plus the $340 million of additional value created by the staging of the purchase.[2]

Engineering Opportunity 2: Set an upper limit on the purchase price. We fully understand that given the competitive nature of acquisitions, delaying the full purchase is not always possible. However, OE valuation can still be used to calculate what the maximum price is that the buyer should pay, taking into account the uncertainty associated with the volatility of HI's bad debt exposure, and thereby avoid being sucked into a bidding war and paying a higher price than is justified. Absent such a valuation, the upper limit on price lies in guesswork and ego, not an auspicious combination.

---

[2] A staged purchase creates the most additional opportunity value (OV) if the acquirer has the right, but not the obligation, to purchase the remainder of the target at a predetermined fixed price at some future time. If the future price is instead based on a multiple of the target company's earnings rather than a fixed price, a common provision, OV is still created, but it is diminished because the asymmetry of the return profile is lessened because the price of the acquisition increases along with the value. A way to counter this is to extend the length of time that the acquirer has to complete the purchase. The longer the time frame, the larger the value of the option to delay, for the obvious reason that it provides the purchaser with more time to evaluate market conditions without being exposed to them.

Engineering Opportunity 3: Opportunity to abandon. Another source of value that can be engineered is to create AV through finding ways to abandon the acquisition in whole or in part. In all probability, HI will have a salvage value if a disappointed HSBC decides to sell it off in the future. This creates AV for the acquisition because it generates the right, but not the obligation, to achieve that salvage value, so the AV thus created needs to be included in the price of the acquisition.

Let's take the negotiated price of approximately ten times earnings and assume that the credit losses at HI turn out to be worse than expected or the consumer interest in having credit cards in the emerging economies is considerably less than expected. The resale value of HI value would still be substantial, although certainly not as much as HSBC paid for it. For the sake of discussion, let's assume that the value falls to eight times earnings, and that due to losses in HI's U.S. loan portfolio, earnings fall to $1 billion from the original $1.4 billion. That would, of course, be unfortunate, and the value of HI would fall to $8 billion from the purchase price of $14 billion. This can be looked upon in two ways. The traditional way is to say that this would mean that the maximum loss HSBC could suffer is $6 billion. But, this is a *salvage* value, not AV. AV adds to the value of the target company because it represents up front the option to abandon the investment. Look at it this way: Acquisitions A and B are the same in every respect except that you can sell off A's assets for $10 million if it fails, and you cannot get a nickel for B's assets if it fails. Which would you pay more for? Thus, AV is additive to the acquisition's value. Our point is that salvage value is not additive; it decreases the cost of failure, but that is different from AV, which stems from holding the option to capture the salvage value.[3]

---

[3] If this seems arcane, let's take an example from the financial markets. If we hold the shares of a stock, we can always sell them, but that ability does not increase their value unless their price rises above their cost. Simple enough. Instead, let's imagine that we have a put option on those shares, meaning that we have the right but not the obligation to sell the stock in the future at the purchase price. That option has value even if the stock price does not move because it protects us if the price falls, because we have the right to sell the shares at their purchase price.

Returning to our example, OE would value the potential application of the HI expertise to emerging markets over the next several decades as an option to expand the operations of HI, whose strike price is the $14 billion paid for the HI acquisition plus investment. John Bond said that this was HSBC's real purpose for acquiring the company. The challenge would be how to design signals into the plan that would indicate whether the acquisition is on track with regard to emerging markets. The earliest signals would probably come from tracking the assumptions made about the consumer credit market in Hungary. OE would require that the assumptions concerning Hungarian consumer behavior be tested frequently against real data to confirm whether management's assumptions are on track. If they are not on track in Hungary, there should be a real question as to whether they will be on track in China and India. To our way of thinking, a failure in Hungary should signal a broader issue that should bring about a serious discussion about selling HI to at least reap the AV.

HSBC and the Engineered Growth Portfolio

The HI acquisition presents an interesting example of how an acquisition can be used to conceive of and create manifold OE projects in an Engineered Growth Portfolio (which we discussed in Chapter 5). HI can be used to create opportunities in all five categories of the portfolio.

1. The IP associated with the HI business in the United States should be considered to represent a rich source of New product Opportunities to HSBC.

2. The potential to expand HI lending expertise to the Asian markets certainly represents myriad Long Reach Opportunities because of the need to develop or acquire the relevant databases and the uncertainty surrounding Asian consumer lending in general as well as the enormous potential.

3. The possibility of expanding the core lending activities of HSBC by passing middle-income loan requests to HI rather than rejecting them out of hand would represent a new market for the bank and should therefore be considered as New Market Opportunities.

4. If the merger is successful in integrating the two companies, these opportunities will form Growth Pathways because they provide the potential to extend HSBC's capabilities into new areas.

5. Lastly, incorporating HI's sophisticated approach to lending with HSBC's branch system represents a rich source of Core Enhancements for the bank.

In general, the more opportunity categories of the Engineered Growth Portfolio that an acquisition touches, the more valuable it is as a strategic investment.

Entering New Markets

By this point, the notion that entry into new markets can create significant EV should not be a surprise. Every new market has uncertainties associated with it revolving around the basic questions of market demand for a product, price points, the growth rate of the market demand for a product, distribution channels, customer service requirements, and so on. OE trains managers to embrace the uncertainties and design the entry into the market in a way that will provide early signals that confirm that the original assumptions remain valid.

Consider an example from the service industry. In 2000, the package delivery service UPS sought to expand its operations to take advantage of the opportunities stemming from the globalization of markets that went beyond carrying packages. The company entered a new market that it calls "insourcing." This is where UPS is invited inside companies to manage a new form of collaboration to create value for both UPS and its customers. For Nike, UPS handles the company's inventory and warehouse for online orders that actually come into UPS, where its UPS employees handle the order taking, payment, pick, pack, and ship functions out of its Kentucky facilities.[4] Another new market opportunity presented itself in Latin America and Europe where UPS expanded its service offering to its traditional shipping clients to the point where it now sends out its own employees to provide service and repairs for Hewlett-Packard printers. These early successes led UPS to offer complete logistics to its customers, which prompted the company to invest $1 billion acquiring logistics companies. UPS, at this point, even handles vehicle delivery for Ford, cutting delivery time from an unpredictable four weeks to ten days on average by redesigning the entire route structure of deliveries.[5] The point is that there would be no way to value these new market opportunities with conventional financial metrics because the uncertainty would most likely render the present value to be nonexistent or worse, thus resulting in a false negative. Intuitively, these market extensions make sense, and we are quite sure that UPS began tentatively with one company and then extended that success to its other customers. If UPS had several choices of which markets to pursue, however, they would need some way to prioritize them with projections of the financial returns that could be expected from each market. This is where OE can prove very useful because of its capability to provide an analytical approach to market selection. We have had clients who have used OE to select between markets in various countries to determine the optimal rollout strategy for a new product.

---

[4] Thomas L. Friedman, *The World is Flat* (New York: Farrar, Straus Gutman, 2006), 169.

[5] Ibid., 173

Opportunity Engineering in Major Contract Negotiations

Almost any clause in a contract that creates or reduces future flexibility for one of the parties is highly likely to have some option value. Think about it: If you can value each of these clauses but your opposing party cannot, you have considerable negotiating advantage.

Often, contracts allow the buyer to purchase additional product at some point in the future at the same price as the initial contract. This is, of course, a good thing for the seller, unless the spot price of the product has gone up in the open market in the meantime because of cost increases or scarcity. Think of a shipping company that was guaranteeing its customers additional capacity on its tankers if they needed it. What is important here is the Opportunity Engineering mindset change that led them to realize that the option on additional capacity could be valued separately and that they could offer the opportunity to price the option separately as an addition to the base contract.

The converse also applies when a company "sells" the option to abandon capacity. In commercial real estate, building owners will sometimes agree to a provision that allows a tenant to extend the lease for an additional length of time after the base lease ends. This provision is routine, and there is some sort of negotiated increase in the rental rate for the space to make up for higher costs on the part of the owner. This provision is, in fact, an option that can be priced because the tenant is not obligated to extend the lease, but the building owner is bound to do so. If the cost of office space declines during the course of the base lease, the tenant will not exercise the renewal clause, choosing instead to lease elsewhere at a lower rate, or the tenant will in all likelihood negotiate a renewal at the lower market rates. On the other hand, if rents rise, the tenant will be motivated to exercise the option to renew the lease. This option could be easily valued, and that provides the opportunity to sell it to the tenant as an addition to the base lease so that the building owner is paid for taking the risk that rents will change.

Another type of contract clause allows the buyer to escape from a contract early. This provides the buyer with the option to abandon the contract, which is, in effect, a put. Staying with commercial real estate as an example, sometimes fast-growing tenants will want the right but not the obligation to terminate the lease early if they need more space but the building owner cannot accommodate their needs. This is a difficult provision for the building owner to live with, but it could be explicitly valued as a put option and sold to the tenant as a separate provision. Being able to provide tenants with this sort of flexibility could be a significant advantage in attracting tenants who are not sure of their future needs, while providing the building owner with adequate compensation for the risk.

On a larger scale, Airbus provides airlines with a similar option that allows an airline to change or cancel aircraft orders.[6] Because of the long lead times in the aircraft industry, the airlines might not want delivery when scheduled, because of a cyclical downturn in passenger demand, or they might want a different aircraft. Airbus sells them the right to defer delivery for a period of time, because the price of the option is less expensive than taking delivery of unneeded airliners.

OE allows the unbundling of contract clauses by pricing them explicitly as options to change contract terms and selling them as such.

Knowing what the options are worth provides the contract negotiators with valuable insight into the value of the contract clauses, and this insight can guide negotiations and provide management with a tool to gauge the effectiveness of its negotiating staff.

---

[6] Peter Coy, "Exploiting Uncertainty, The 'Real Options' Revolution in Decision Making," *Business Week*, June 7, 1999.

Research and Development

We have touched on the power of using OE in R&D projects in examples throughout the book, so we will not dwell on it in depth. By this time, we hope that it is clear that many of the inefficiencies that occur in new product and process development result from using the wrong tools to select, manage, and value highly uncertain R&D investments. NPV alone just cannot value projects when the uncertainty surrounding them is high because there is no logical way to forecast the amount, nor the timing of cash flows, which are nebulous to begin with. The effect of OE on R&D proposals will be to enhance value where appropriate. In most cases, the discipline of OE in conjunction with Discovery Driven Planning (DDP) will lead to more aggressive investments in upside potential, while controlling risk.

Opportunity Engineering used with the EVS software, which is discussed in detail in the next chapter, can be used to back into allowable expenses that can be very useful in project planning and ongoing management. Let's take an example where the cost of R&D for a new IT service was an estimated $70,000, and the project had acceptable returns, but there was not a great deal of confidence surrounding the estimated cost. As a result, management wanted to know the maximum that could be spent on R&D. In practice, we find this exercise to be immensely useful, because the question always arises as to whether R&D will in the end generate value for a company. It is often quite difficult to know the answer because of the uncertainty surrounding the projections. Our approach helps overcome these difficulties because our software accepts distributions of outcomes to generate project values.

Let's take a look at how this might work. In this example, we varied only the R&D budget and held all the other inputs concerning the project such as market size, timing, competitive response, cost of plant and equipment, and expected margins constant to back into the maximum that could be spent on R&D. We replaced the original estimate of $70,000 with $200,000 in the model and ran the numbers, again holding all else constant, we then put in $400,000, $600,000, $800,000, and finally $1,000,000 as the R&D budget. Figure 6.3 shows the results.

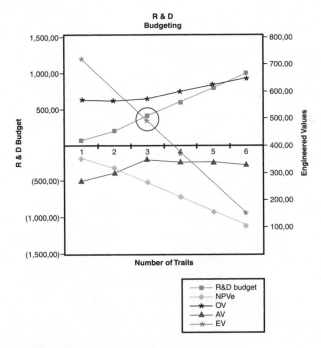

Figure 6.3 Using OE as a budgeting tool

The left vertical axis shows the R&D budget, which is shown as the ascending line. The axis on the right is the Engineered Value. The other lines on the chart depict the changes in NPVe, OV, AV, and EV. The NPVe line descends along with the increase in R&D spending, which makes sense because NPV is the present value of the expected future returns minus the investment needed to generate those returns. Therefore, if we hold all inputs constant, we have fixed the present value of the project. Now if we increase the investment in R&D, we change the NPV of the project, because we are subtracting a larger number. As you see from the divergence of the R&D line and the NPV line, the relationship is pretty close to linear. This brings to light the fact that traditional analysis leading to NPV really is not much help with early-stage projects because there are too many sources of uncertainty to be accounted for in one number. The learning from this chart lies elsewhere.

At the third iteration (number 3 on the horizontal axis, which relates to $400,000 of R&D spending), we see the R&D budget line cross the EV line. That intersection signals the maximum amount that should reasonably be spent on the R&D effort. At that point, the components of project value are as follows:

R&D budget = $400,000
NPVe   = –$510,000
OV   = $650,000
AV   = $350,000
EV   = $490,000

In our view, when the R&D budget, which represents a potential real loss, nears the EV of the project, it signals the maximum that should be spent on R&D. At that point, you are balancing a real cost against a potential gain, which we think represents a boundary. If we were advising a company on a project that had these characteristics, we would suggest that the R&D budget should not exceed that shown at the second trial when R&D = $200,000 and the EV = $600,000. That sort of a ratio is much more comfortable because it provides a cushion. In general, the more uncertain a project is, the greater the ratio between EV and R&D should be. The same logic applies to any other stage of a project. For instance, it would be easy to determine the maximum that could be spent building a plant or distribution system in light of the potential markets a new product is expected to reach.

Before we leave this discussion, the line depicting AV merits a brief explanation. As you can see, it tracks up slightly as we increase R&D spending. This is to be expected because as we increase the R&D budget we increase the odds that the project will fail and we are more likely to seek out the AV that was built in to the project at the outset. As a result, holding on to an option to abandon has more value.

Strategic Planning under Uncertainty

We essentially view strategic planning as presenting a series of options to companies. At its most basic level, strategy is based on expectations that the market and the competition will respond in a certain way to the initiating firm's actions. Often, however, it is impossible to know with precision whether the market and competition will respond as anticipated, because by definition there is a great deal of uncertainty in any strategy. That uncertainty translates into option value, which is captured with OE but glossed over with traditional management and valuation techniques. The option comes directly from the range of possible competitive responses to the strategy, some of which are beneficial and some of which are not. The key benefit of using OE with strategic planning is that it allows managers to plan the optimum strategy using decision trees and probabilities to generate the values for each strategy and anticipated competitive response. This serves as an excellent selection tool to arrive at the best strategy, and it also brings about a more flexible mindset on the part of strategists and managers, who by the very nature of the exercise learn to think through contingency plans to every response to the strategy.

Consider an example from the reported strategy of the cigarette wars in the early 1990s, when on April 2, 1993 ("Marlboro Friday"), Philip Morris announced a 20% price reduction on Marlboro—its premium brand—in the United States, accompanied by a massive increase in advertising. R.J. Reynolds Tobacco Company (R.J. Reynolds) responded by matching prices and boosting advertising in the United States. Within three months, both firms were back at their original market shares but at much reduced prices. Why did Philip Morris cut prices only to return to original shares at a much lower margin? The real game for Philip Morris was not the American market at all. The real game was in the free Central European markets, which had just been released from Soviet domination and were now ripe for American cigarettes. The problem was that Philip Morris was late to the party, so it now had to chase R.J. Reynolds, which was in the lead. The strategic choices were head-to-head combat in Central Europe or something less direct but potentially more effective, if it worked. Philip Morris cut prices on Marlboro cigarettes by a dramatic 20% because they believed R.J. Reynolds would have to respond to save the market share of their premium brand Winston cigarettes. But R.J. Reynolds was strapped for cash at the time, and they could not defend the U.S. market and continue to expand in Central Europe, so the company would have to make a choice. Philip Morris bet that R.J. Reynolds would defend their Winston brand in the United States, giving Philip Morris time to get its plans pulled together for Central Europe. In this example, we see the interplay of strategic options. The first option was how R.J. Reynolds would respond to the attack. They could have done nothing, in which case Philip Morris would have lost a lot of money by having cut the price of Marlboro cigarettes while simultaneously ramping up advertising spending. Alternatively, R.J. Reynolds could have come out swinging, which is what they did. The uncertainties lay with the degree of response from R.J. Reynolds, the length of the campaign in the U.S. market, the cost of entering the Central European markets, the success in gaining market share in Central Europe, and so on. If you don't think of this strategy as a set of options, what is it?

Managing Not-for-Profit Projects

We have couched this book in terms of for-profit business because that is the world that we work in, yet discussions with a leading scientist doing government-sponsored research alerted us to the notion that OE is just as important in effectively managing not-for-profit projects. Here, the problem is the discontinuity between the mountain of requests for research grants and the paucity of funding. When researchers petition governmental and nongovernmental organizations for funds, they usually plan the project from beginning to end, spend all the money, and wait to see the results. If the project works as intended, they get useful data that can sometimes influence legislation, especially in the natural sciences. If the project does not work as intended, they learn little but spent a lot of money. This is much like project management in the private sector, except it probably has less oversight. Would it not be better to use the principles found in this book to help manage research in a more cost-effective manner? The same principles used to manage uncertain projects in the private sector are just as effective in managing scientific research. It was suggested to us that the discipline of listing the assumptions that lie behind a research project and then designing CheckPoints to test their veracity as early as possible would be enormously useful because scientists are prone to ignoring information that does not confirm their belief structure. Why let disappointing projects run their full course, spending all the money, when they could be terminated early and have the resources redirected to a more promising project? We recognize that this would require a change in mindset on the part of researchers and their funding organizations that would have to allow funds to be switched from one project to another. We also understand that this would not be an inconsequential task, but we hope that Opportunity Engineering could help achieve this higher level of efficiency.

In the next chapter, we look at the how to value projects in detail and explain how to interpret the numbers and use the software to build more Engineered Value into your projects.

7

Project Valuation Using EVS Software

In this chapter, we get into the specifics of valuing projects using the EVS software. Even though in our view, valuation is secondary to the Opportunity Engineering, valuation is useful for choosing among competing projects, because understanding the value components comprising a project allows you to select the very best investments from a number of choices.

So, the first benefit is that if you have a portfolio of potential investments, it makes sense to focus on those that promise the most Opportunity Value (OV), and among these the ones with the highest net present value (NPVe).

Our EVS software has other uses, too. And as the chapter progresses, we show you these, but let's start with the simplest application (just specifying the project in OE terms) and do the valuation.

We are not going to demonstrate the detailed nuts and bolts of how to actually use the EVS software. This is demonstrated in detail in the online demo tutorial that you can access by going to our website, www.oppengine.com. The software is proprietary, and it can be licensed. It is not associated with Wharton Publishing.

As usual, we illustrate the basics using an example, starting with an exposition of a simple R&D project with a relatively intractable valuation challenge.

R&D Project Example

As a starting point, let's consider a project that has the following characteristics:

- *Undertake R&D* at a cost of $2,000,000, with an estimated 50% probability that at the R&D CheckPoint the R&D will succeed.

- If the research effort is successful, the company will *test market* the proposed product, which it thinks will have a 60% chance of success at the test market CheckPoint.

- If the test market is *successful,* the company can apply for a patent. At the patent completed CheckPoint, there is an estimated 50% chance that it will be awarded, and it will take three to four years to get the patent.

- After the patent is decided, the firm can build a manufacturing facility for between $4 to $7 million, with an expected cost of $4.5 million (they have no experience with this type of plant), that will yield net revenues that depend on expected competitive response.

  If the *patent is unsuccessful,* and the company builds the plant and enters the market *without patent protection,* there will be a rapid competitive response, with rapidly eroded sales and market share. In this case, *total net revenue yield* is expected to be about $3 million but could range from $2.0 to $4.0 million.

  However if the *patent is successful,* management thinks that they can hold the competition at bay for ten years before they start to face competitive erosion of profits. In this case, the *total net revenue yield from operations* is expected to be $5.0 million, but this could range from $2 to $8.5 million—in other words, the project has highly uncertain net revenues, with high upside potential.

Again, we will not take you through the mechanics of how the modeling is done using the EVS software because that is covered in the online tutorial.

Figure 7.1 shows how the EVS software distills the R&D project into an event tree.

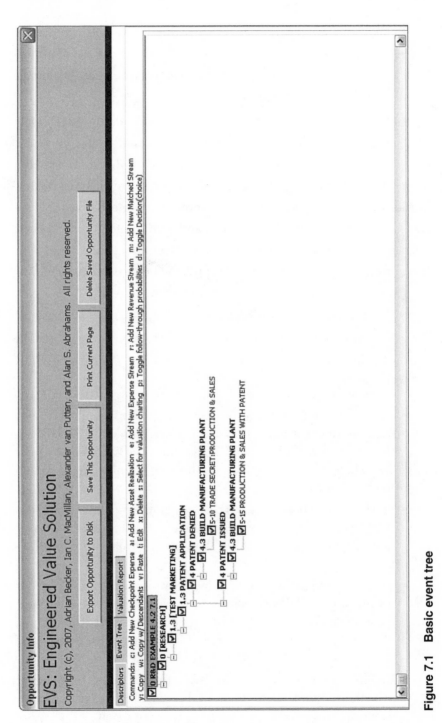

Figure 7.1   Basic event tree

In an event-tree diagram, you lay out the different possible paths of events that must occur as the project unfolds from CheckPoint to CheckPoint. No branch of an event tree can occur if the CheckPoint event before it has not occurred.

In Figure 7.1, you can see that first you need to do the R&D. Only when this is done do you do the test marketing, and only when this is done do you apply for the patent. Next, fate decides whether you get the patent or not. If it is denied, you can elect to build the plant and manufacture without a patent, hoping to be somewhat protected by trade secret. On the other hand, if you are lucky and get the patent, you can build the plant and commence production, with sales under patent protection. In the software, you input associated probabilities, quantities, and timing, the details of which are covered in the online tutorial.

We call this an event tree because the project is displayed as a series of *outcomes* rather than decisions. We intentionally made it look like a decision tree because that is familiar to many managers, but it differs in several important ways:

- First and foremost, it causes managers to think of all the things that can or must *happen* as the project unfolds. It makes you think in terms of necessary CheckPoint *results* for a path to occur, which immediately has you thinking about what we can *do* to engineer that path.

- Second, it teaches managers that designing the path to keep options open and remaining flexible has real value, and that value needs to be preserved rather than prematurely shutting off alternatives.

- Third, related to the second, it helps prevent a need for false determinism from taking hold, which can create pressure to opt for a single course of action before it is warranted. The process of creating an event tree in and of itself engenders discussions about what could happen, or could be made to happen.

- Finally, this type of modeling obviates the need to arrive at probability estimates for unknowable events, which is (often ludicrously) required with a decision tree approach.

When you run the valuation of the event tree, you get Figure 7.2 for the valuation of the first cut at the project.

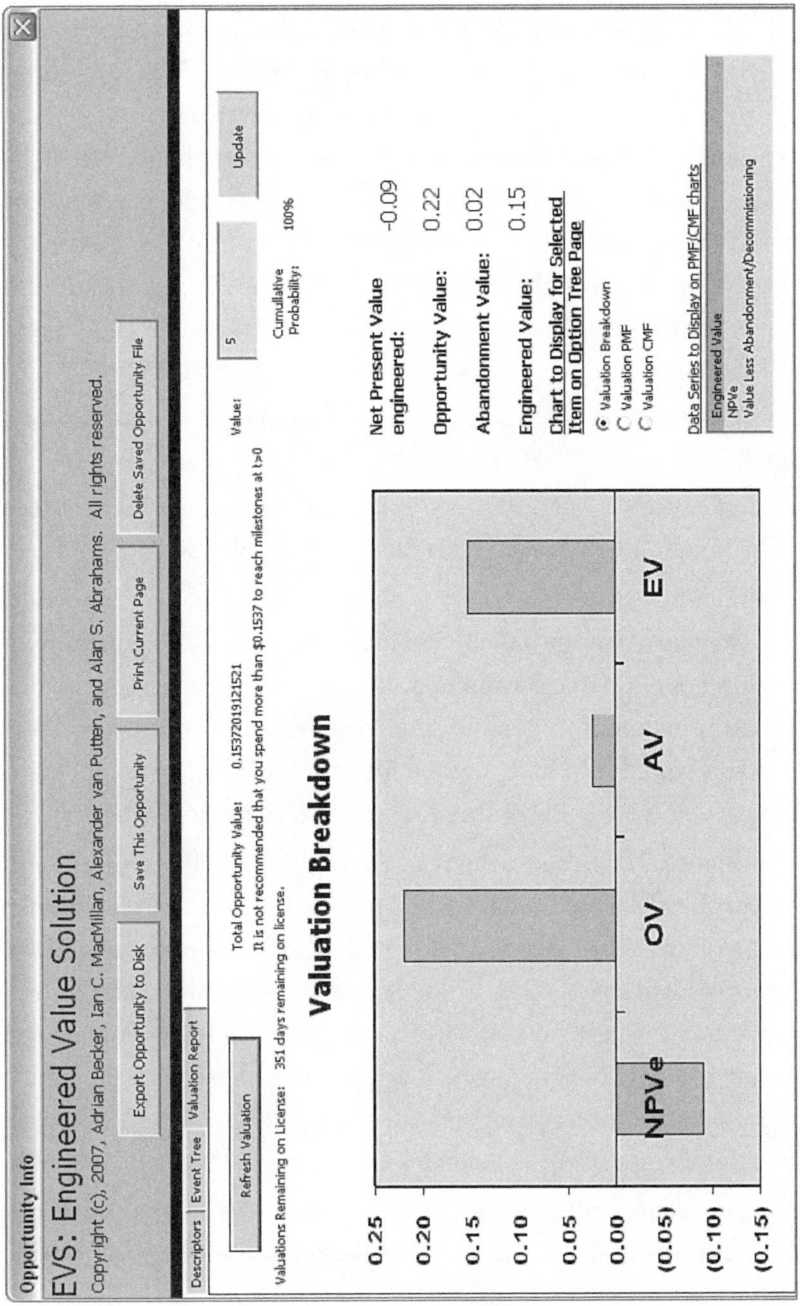

Figure 7.2   Basic valuation breakdown

Figure 7.2 shows how the software breaks out the different components of value as a summary of the project valuation components for the project modeled in Figure 7.1.

In the lower left, you can see we used a required rate of return of 15%. Based on this required rate, the key numbers are listed in columnar format on the column on the right side the chart, where we see the most likely values of each value component in millions of dollars: NPVe is negative 0.09, opportunity value (OV) is 0.22, abandonment value (AV) is 0.02, so the final Engineered Value (EV) is 0.15 (that is $150,000), with the bulk coming from OV. The EVS software also shows these same value components in histogram form in the left center of the figure.

With an NPVe = –$90,000, this project would be killed stone dead from the get-go. *But…*let's do some Opportunity Engineering! Before we take the project out and shoot it, let's consider what other sources of value might be engineered into this project that have not yet been considered.

First, what if we "go naked" and build the plant without patenting, (thus foregoing the patent protection), entering the market immediately and beginning to generate net revenues after positive market tests? This would lead to decreased total revenues due to competitive response, *but* we would get these revenues three years earlier!

In Figure 7.3 we show the revised event tree, which is the same basic graphical depiction that we had before, but now there is another branch coming off of Test Marketing that drops down to Build Manufacturing Plant followed by Trade Secret Production & Sales immediately after the test marketing. This layers in the first engineered alternative course of action, which is just going ahead with the building of a manufacturing plant and launching the product right after a successful market study instead of waiting for a patent to be issued.

Again, via the software, this new project design and its event tree can be reconfigured and calculated in fractions of minutes.

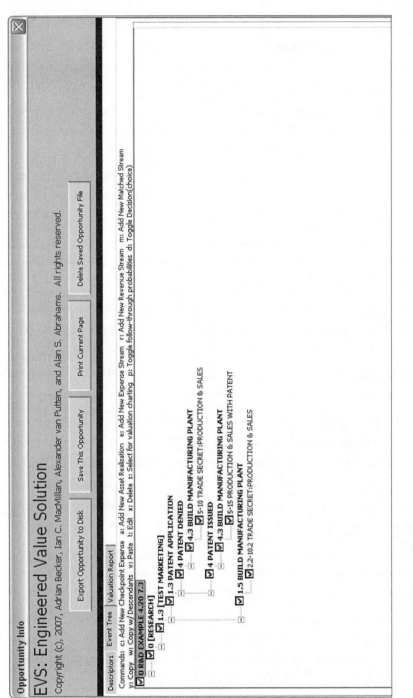

Figure 7.3   No Patent event tree

Now that you are getting familiar with the charts, let's look at Figure 7.3 in a little more detail. In front of each named branch of the event tree is a square with a check mark in it. The check mark instructs the software to use the checked branch in the valuation. If you uncheck it, it will ignore that branch and any subbranch following that unchecked branch. Therefore, you (and anyone to whom you are presenting or planning with) can see what happens to value as you "shut off" or "turn on" alternatives. This capability allows rapid valuations of "what ifs" stemming from discussions of variations of the project.

Figure 7.4 shows what adding the engineered alternative of going forward without a patent does to the valuation. (Again this can be calculated by the EVS software in a fraction of a minute.)

Adding this flexibility changes the value of the project substantially. Now the NPVe has moved from negative $90,000 up to $80,000, the OV decreased to $190,000, and the AV increased to $220,000. As a result, the EV of the project is increased to $490,000, with a positive NPVe to boot. This makes the proposition much more attractive.

Let's do some further Opportunity Engineering. Suppose the team suggests something really heretical for a typical manufacturing firm mindset: What if, after demonstrating feasibility in the lab, we just sell the IP we have developed and not even bother about test marketing, applying for a patent, or building a plant? The heretical team estimates that this could lead to a sale of the IP for between $2.8 to $3.8 million, with a most likely IP selling price of $3 million.

Where does this IP selling price come from? Remember that by the time you have a successful R&D project to sell, you are selling something that originally cost $2 million to develop, and with originally only a 50% chance of success. The IP purchaser is now being offered a proven successful technical outcome (in other words, 100% chance of success). If there is disagreement with this IP price range, the beauty about the EVS software is that it takes no more than fractions of a minute to input and run well-argued alternative price ranges.

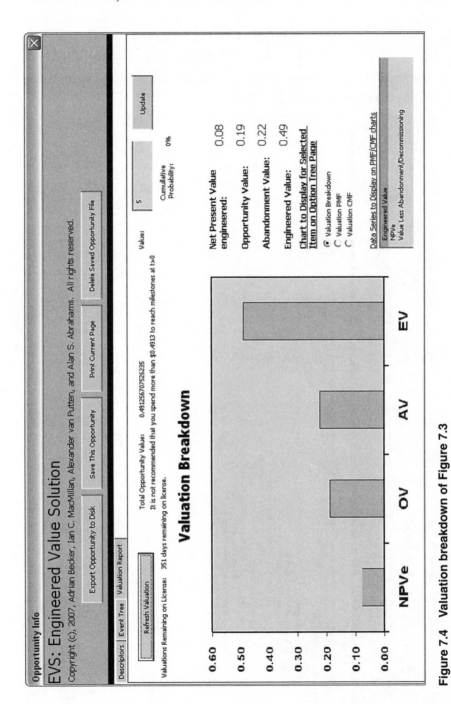

Figure 7.4   Valuation breakdown of Figure 7.3

Figure 7.5 shows how this additional Opportunity Engineering play can be layered into the original event tree, and Figure 7.6 shows how the EVS software gives you a recalculation of component values within fractions of a minute.

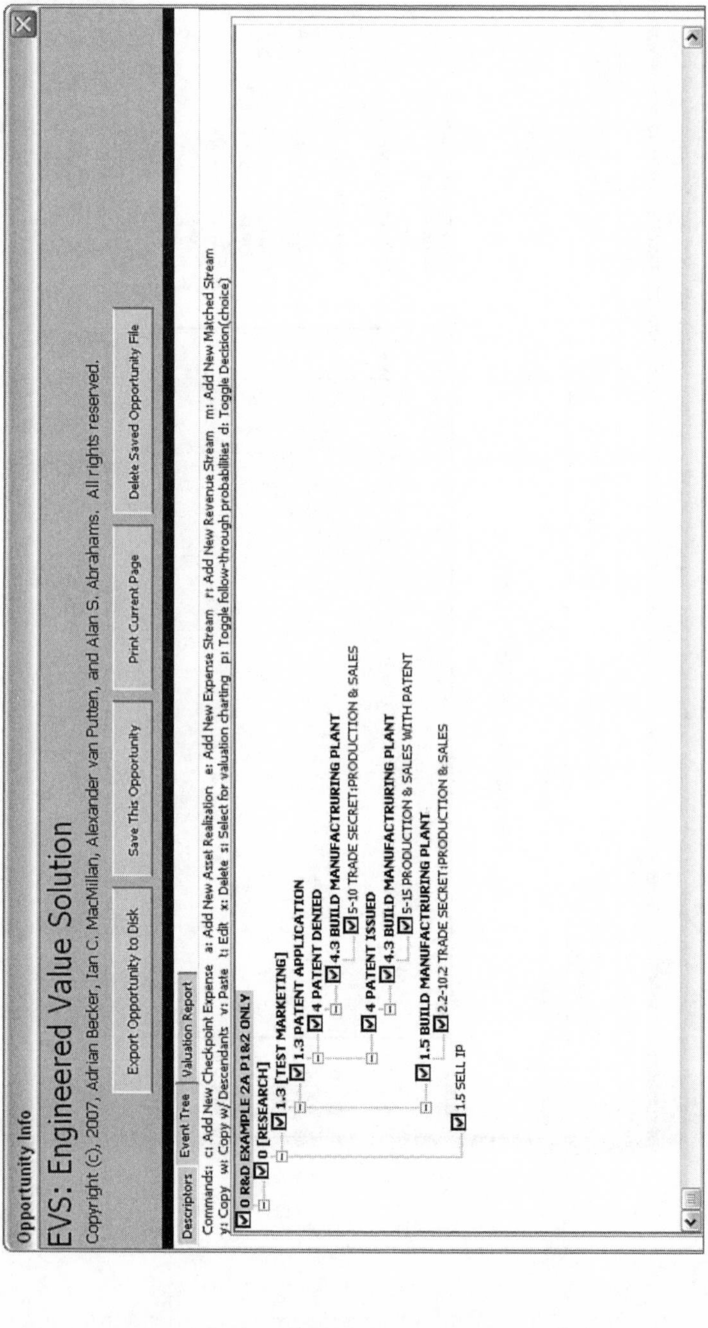

Figure 7.5   Sell IP event tree

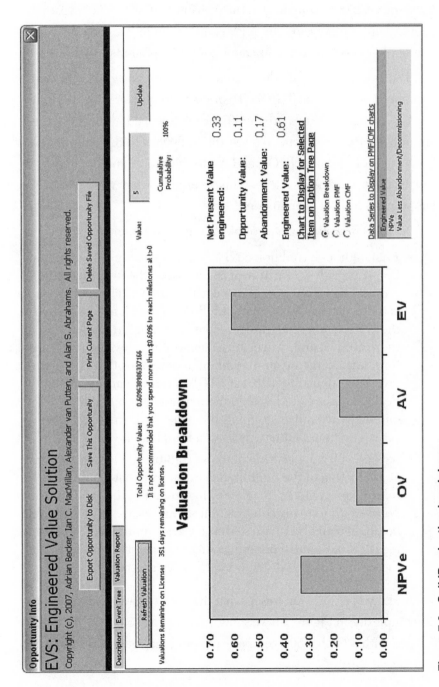

Figure 7.6 Sell IP valuation breakdown

After engineering in the flexibility of selling off the IP, the project now has the same EV of $490,000, but it has a much-improved NPVe of $330,000 compared to the previous $80,000. The investment engineering is increasing the NPVe and depending less on the more-intangible opportunity and abandonment components of value.

The overall effect of adding more flexibility to the project development plan (that is, selling the IP or going to market without IP protection) is that there is a greater chance of succeeding because there are now four ways to win. We see this reflected in the shift of value from the more intangible OV and AV to the more tangible, thanks to substantially increased NPVe. This is exactly what we want to see happen as a project is engineered.

Now we want to make a couple of important points:

- First, although traditional NPV analysis yields a valuation number, it provides no real insight into what the key uncertainties are, and therefore how to manage the project. The real problem is that a classic discounted cash flow approach used to arrive at the NPV models the project from beginning to end, as though there is no flexibility to change course along the way. It is, therefore, just averaging all the potential outcomes that could arise, given the inputs, to arrive at a NPV. Here we are baking in the flexibility associated with pursuing not one but four possible outcomes, as well as stopping all further investment in the project at any time that fate deals us a bum hand!

- Second, it is hugely difficult to use traditional methods to arrive at a valuation of the multibranch event tree that would be helpful to management. Imagine trying to model this project using NPV? With so many combinations of inputs, the best that could be done would be to use a Monte Carlo simulation to get some idea of the spread of potential outcomes, and then present value the average of that distribution to arrive at a proxy for NPV.

And if you really want to see what the EVS software can do to handle complexity, in Figure 7.9 we show a *part* of an event tree that we developed with a Global 500 company to help it navigate and engineer a multibillion-dollar, staged investment that was just seething with uncertainty. Want to try to do an NPV analysis of this project that makes any sense? As they would say in Brooklyn, New York, "Fuggeddaboudit!"

Valuing "What If" Future Events

So far, we have been looking at the project at time zero (that is, *at the beginning, before we have spent any money*). Using the EVS, it is a simple matter to project ourselves into the future and probe the effect that later learning might have on the project.

For instance, what if, after spending the money on R&D, we get to the end of the test marketing and find that we need to adjust our revenue estimates down by 20%? Would the project be a complete disaster, or would we still be okay? Wouldn't it be nice to know this *before* we have spent a nickel on the R&D?

We can easily take a look by changing the revenue assumptions in the model and valuing the project from the test-marketing step onward. Figure 7.7 shows the resulting output.

The valuation breakdown histogram in Figure 7.7 has an additional bar marked SC, which shows the sunk costs that would have been incurred to get to that point in the project. In this example, we would have already spent $2 million on the research and a bit more on the market test (which is rounded away in the output). EVS, by default, deducts the sunk costs from the EV to arrive at $370,000. This basically says that if we go ahead and spend money on R&D and test marketing, even if the market projections are 20% lower, we will not regret going ahead and building the plant—and we know this even before spending on the R&D!

The same kind of analysis can be done for any event, and for any time, to provide as complete of a look into the future merits of a project as possible. In addition to providing insightful sensitivity analyses, this exercise quickly isolates the key drivers that underpin the project's economic returns.

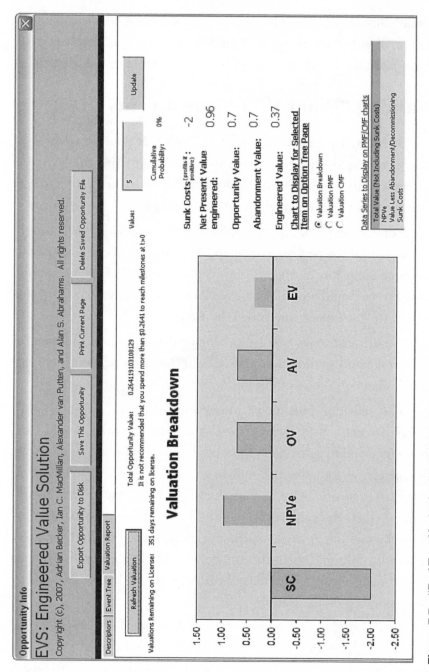

Figure 7.7 "Bad Test Marketing" valuation breakdown

Other EVS Functions

The EVS valuation breakdowns we have shown provide a summary of all the component values that the project could yield, but these numbers on the valuation breakdown are the expected, or most likely, outcomes.

For uncertain investments, there is a *range* of possible outcomes clustered around these most likely values shown in the valuation breakdowns, and you need to be aware of the breadth of these ranges. An EV of 4 that can range from 0 to 8 might be preferable to an EV of 6 that could range from minus 4 to 12! You might not have the cash reserves to suck up the minus 4.

So, in addition to the valuation numbers from the valuation breakdown reports, EVS provides information about the range of the EV for a project, (or, for any major event tree within the project).

Cumulative Mass Function of EV

To give you an indication of the range of possible results, an alternative view of the EV of our project is shown in the Cumulative Mass Function (CMF) chart in Figure 7.8.

Figure 7.8 shows similar data to that found in Figure 7.6 but in terms of probabilities of outcome.

In the cumulative probability chart in Figure 7.8, the range of possible EVs of the project is shown along the horizontal axis in million-dollar increments. So, the value of 1 along the horizontal axis represents $1 million of EV.

The cumulative probability of each value is shown along the vertical axis. So what the vertical number on the graph shows is the probability that the project has less value than the value on the horizontal x-axis.

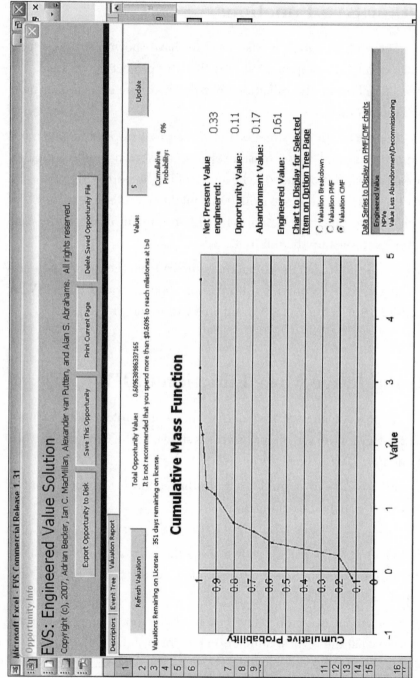

Figure 7.8 Cumulative probability chart

So, take the value of 1 on the x-axis (representing EV of $1 million) and imagine a vertical line drawn from 1 up to intersect the graph line. Imagine a horizontal line drawn left from this intersection with the graph. This cuts the y-axis at about 0.9, which says that there is a 90% chance that the project would yield a value of $1 million or less.

Now look at the value of zero (0) on the x-axis. Projecting up we see the graph line intersects at a y-axis value of about 1.5, which means there is a 15% chance you will make less than zero, or in other words, a loss.

*But...*now look at where the graphs ends on the left: the value on the horizontal axis of about –0.15, which has an 11% chance. This shows that the most you can lose is $110,000, and there is only an 11% chance of losing this much!

Finally, look at where the graph ends on the right, which is $5 million dollars at 100%. This says you can make no more than $5 million (100% chance of less than $5 million).

So, overall, the Cumulative Mass Function graph says that although the expected value of the project is $610,000, there is a 15% probability of losing money, but the most you can lose is $110,000, with an 11% chance, and the most you can make is $5 million.

In this case, we see that the Opportunity Engineered project is not too risky even though 30% of the potential returns are below zero, because the downside is not more than a $250,000 loss (including the R&D!), and the upside could go as high as $5 million. The team has truly engineered the project!

The lesson here is that it is imperative to consider both the most likely value of EV and the CMF chart, which shows the range of values. Without the CMF view, it is possible to charge after a high-promise, but awfully risky project!

More Complex Projects

We have deliberately kept our example simple to bring out the features of the EVS and to demonstrate that Opportunity Engineering (OE) can lead to a rapid but accurate and meaningful financial valuation.

The software can handle much more complex projects with relative ease. We show in Figure 7.9 the first page of a complex OE financial model that dealt with multiple product designs, multiple markets, and multiple partners to arrive at an almost optimal strategy. We show here only the first page of the model for reasons of confidentiality. The entire model ran several pages, with hundreds of lines of inputs.

We hope that after reading this book you have the sense an alternative way exists to deal with uncertain investments that allow you to engineer bold, profit-spawning projects while containing their risk of a loss to a very narrow range. Even if you never run the numbers using the EVS software, the OE mindset has immense power to change the way you think about all types of investments.

We urge you to bring Opportunity Engineering into your company to see what it can do for you. We have learned that the best way to do so is to Opportunity Engineer one or two pilot projects that face considerable uncertainty and apply the concepts of this book, making sure that you temper your investment appetite with engineered control of your risks. You will be impressed with the results.

If you want to learn more about the software, go to the OE website www.oppengine.com or contact us directly at alexvp@wharton.upenn.edu.

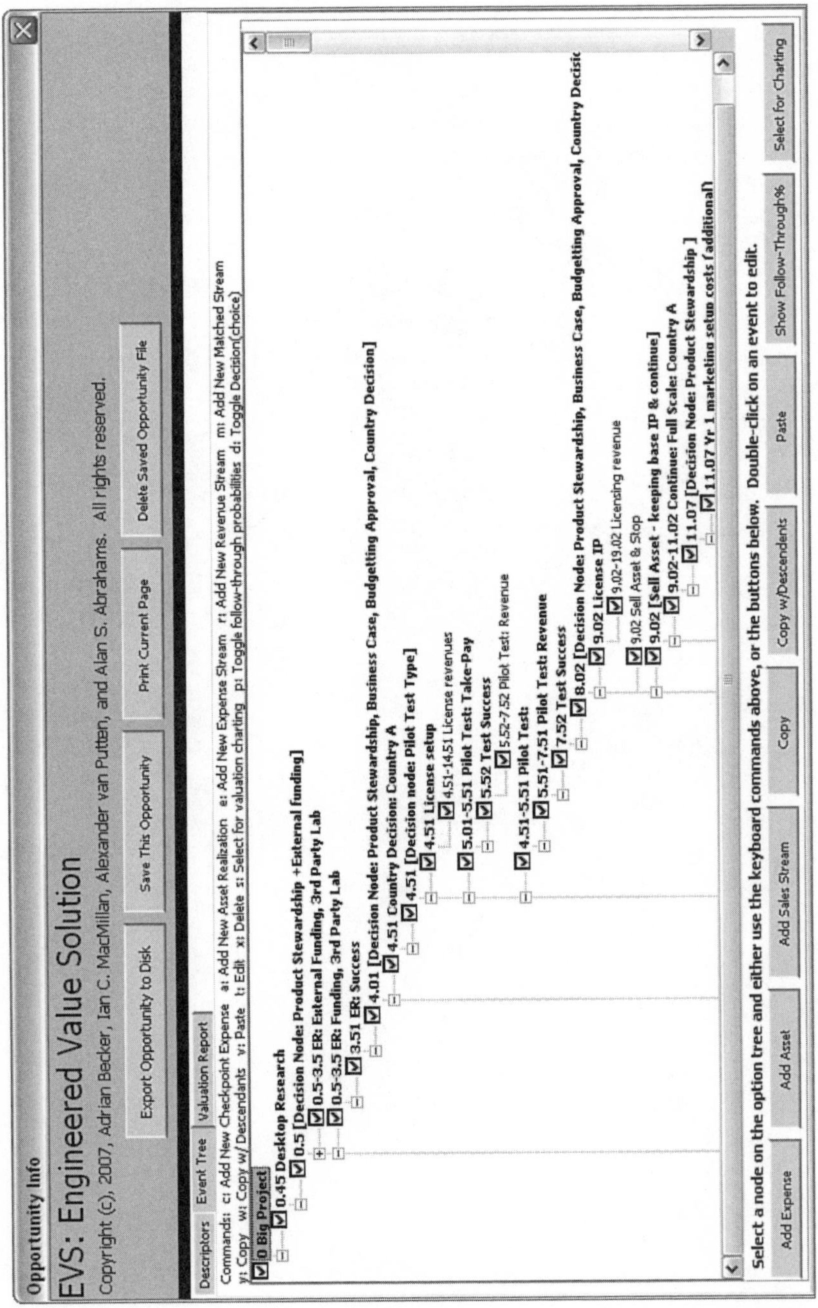

Figure 7.9 Modeling more complexity

Appendix A ————————————

The Underpinnings of the EVS Software

Adrian Becker

Origins of the EVS Approach

Real options valuation as it has existed in recent years has become a byproduct of the following two tools:

- **Decision Tree Analysis**—Where there are discrete points in time when we gain additional information about our underlying value opportunities.
- **Financial Option Valuation**—Where assumptions on the absence of arbitrage and market completeness allow us to disregard any need to risk-adjust cash flows; additionally in financial markets there is justification for modeling underlying assets as well behaved random processes which can be calibrated with historical data.

The key to real option valuation is to recognize how the fact that changing information available to the holder affects the option value over time. So how and when additional information comes to the user is a key assumption in any option valuation model. In financial options, this information gain is modeled through asset prices that change over time according to a diffusion process; in decision tree analysis, all information gained is modeled explicitly and discretely.

Problems with Traditional Approaches

What we have recognized is the following:

- Holders of real options are most comfortable stating a probability distribution for the value of an underlying event at a specific time; however, stating how information gain will affect the future value distribution over time is a difficult and often arbitrarily handled task. For instance, consider trying to model the value of a revenue stream of a new product line as one would a stock for use in Black-Scholes; deriving a volatility associated with such a process would be moot, and there are no underlying assumptions that justify the choice of model.

- Decision Tree modeling is cumbersome and in and of itself an exponentially complex task. For instance, if I have 4 underlying objects for each of which I can gain "Up" or "Down" information at 3 different dates, I would need a tree with $(2^4)^3=4096$ branches. In many instances, our clients come to us with have hundreds of events with varying degrees of uncertainty over long periods of time and having a large number of decision points, making such analysis impossible.

Basis of the EVS Approach

Our option valuation method then lays its foundation on the following simple truisms:

- The value of a real option is bounded above by the "perfect information case." That is, if I know with complete certainty the value that underlying objects will realize, I can always make the best decisions possible, leave nothing to chance, and capture all upside and experience no downside.

- The value of a real option is bounded below by the "no information case." That is, if I will learn nothing more than what I know today, the best estimate for the value of an opportunity is simply the net present value of every possible outcome I am currently considering weighted by the probability that that outcome occurs. (In arbitrage-free financial option valuation, one is simply stating that the "market implies" an appropriate risk-neutral probability distribution.)

The EVS tool enables you to explore the region within these two bounds through an intuitive calibration. The user simply enters a timeline of events (in a tree structure to indicate dependency and mutual exclusivity—the event tree) and a probability distribution associated with each event (there are tools to copy, paste, and move around events quickly to facilitate the development of intricate time-lines). In order to explore the bounds given above, we assume that throughout time for each event we are on independent random walks up and down the stated probability distribution in such a way that at the time each event is realized, the distribution of where we end up matches the stated probability distribution. The speed at which each random walk occurs is governed by input parameters from the user, derived from how often he or she states that estimates will be updated in the real world for each underlying event. Now at any given time when we have to make a decision, we know where we are on each random walk and how fast we are moving on each random walk, so we have the conditional probability distribution for what the actual value of each event will actually be (representing our knowledge gain). Using techniques called quadrature and dynamic programming, we are then able to quickly ascertain the value of very large chains of options under such a model.

The value of the EVS tool, however, is not simply "the number" you get out for the value of an opportunity embedded with options, but more importantly, the ability to see how events in a valued chain interrelate. For instance, all valuations are broken down into NPVe, Abandonment and Added Opportunity Value components, so you can see how much of the stated value is coming from the assumptions imbedded in the model through your input parameters.

Cumulative Probability distributions of value are also given so you do not have to rely on point estimates to make decisions. Once valued, you can also pick any point on the chain and look at the value distribution going forward to see "what the value would be if you got there" and backward to see "how much it would cost to get there."

Furthermore, the likelihood that each available decision will be made in the future is provided, allowing you to focus resources more efficiently and isolate those events for which information gain is most valuable.

Notes

EVS Formulation

Adrian Becker

Definition *We define an <u>event</u> E as a random variable indexed with a time of realization $t_E \in \mathbb{R}_+$ and with a value distribution function $F_E \in L^p(\mathbb{R})$ for some $p \geq 2$. We refer to the value of E at time t_E as the "value at realization".*

Definition *We define an <u>n,m-approximation function</u> $A : \mathbb{R}_+ \times L^p(\mathbb{R}) \rightarrow \mathbb{R}_+ \times (\mathbb{R}^2 \times \mathbb{R}^n)$ as a function that takes an event E and approximates F_E by a discrete distribution of n point masses through a quadrature process which matches the first $m \leq p$ moments of F_E. We will reference each such point mass as a point in $\mathbb{R}^2$ representing a (weight, abscissa) pair, (π_i^E, x_i^E). We refer to the range of of n-approximation function as an approximation event.*

Definition *We define an <u>estimate process</u> $T(E)$ as a stationary continuous-time Markov process with a reference event E. For the reference event, we define an approximation event $\hat{E} = A(E)$. We let the stages of the estimate process be the abscissa $\{x_i\}_{i=1}^n$ and set the initial probability distribution to be $\{\pi_i\}_{i=1}^n$. We then define a tri-diagonal transition-rate matrix Q_T such that transitions from each stage to an adjacent one happen on average once every time unit and such that T is a stationary process. We assume any estimate processes we define live on a common filtered probability space and are independent unless otherwise noted.*

Definition *We define an <u>estimate efficiency function</u> $f_T : \mathbb{R}_+^2 \rightarrow \mathbb{R}_+$ (with reference estimate process T) as a function that maps actual time passage to effective time passage for the process T. That is to say that for any two points in time $t_i < t_j$, the probability transition matrix for the process T is given by $P_T(t_i, t_j) = \exp[Q_T \cdot f_T(t_i, t_j)]$ (here $\exp[\cdot]$ is the matrix exponential function).*

Definition *We define an <u>event chain</u> $(\mathfrak{E}, \mathfrak{D}, \mathfrak{X})$ as a set of events $\mathfrak{E} = \{E_j\}$ equipped with a dependency function $\mathfrak{D} : \mathfrak{E} \rightarrow 2^{\mathfrak{E}}$ and an exclusivity function $\mathfrak{X} : \mathfrak{E} \rightarrow 2^{\mathfrak{E}}$ with the property: $E_j \in \mathfrak{D}(E) \Rightarrow t_{E_j} \leq t_E$, likewise $E_j \in \mathfrak{X}(E) \Rightarrow t_{E_j} \leq t_E$. The set $\mathfrak{D}(E)$ may be viewed as the set of events that must be realized in order for E to be realized. The set $\mathfrak{X}(E)$ may be viewed as the set of events that if realized, prevent E from being realized.*

Definition *We define a <u>decision point</u> as a point in time $t_D \in \mathbb{R}_+$ and a set of events $\Phi_D = \{E_j\}$ such that $t_D \leq t_{E_j} \; \forall j$. This decision point represents the ability to forgo the realization of the events Φ_D at time t_D. For each decision point, we define a control function $u_D(\mathfrak{F}_{t_D})$ which represents whether or not* *the events in Φ_D are forgone based on the information available at time t_D, $u_D(\mathfrak{F}_{t_D}) = 0$ iff the events are forgone, 1 otherwise. Here $\mathfrak{F}_{t_D}$ is the natural filtration at time t_D generated by the estimate processes.*

Definition *We define an <u>option chain</u> as a set of decision points $\{D_k\}$ with $t_{D_k} \leq t_{D_{k+1}}$ and an event chain $\overline{(\mathfrak{C}, \mathfrak{D}, \mathfrak{X})}$ such that $E \in \Phi_{D_k} \Rightarrow E \in \mathfrak{C}$, $\Phi_{D_v} \cap \Phi_{D_w} = \emptyset \; \forall v \neq w$.*

Finally the option chain valuation problem is given to us for some fixed discretezation factor n and an option chain $\{D_k\}, (\mathfrak{C}, \mathfrak{D}, \mathfrak{X})$ as deriving the optimal control functions $\{u_{D_k}(\mathfrak{F}_{t_{D_k}})\}$ that solve the following dynamic program:

$$J_k = \mathbb{E}\left[\max_{\{u_{D_k}(\mathfrak{F}_{t_{D_k}})\}}\left(J_{k+1} + u_{D_k}(\mathfrak{F}_{t_{D_k}}) \cdot \sum_{E \in \Phi_{D_k}} T(E)_{t_E} \cdot \eta(E)\right) \bigg| \mathfrak{F}_{t_{D_k}}\right]$$

$$J_{Terminal} = \mathbb{E}\left[\sum_{E \in \mathfrak{N}} T(E)_{t_E} \cdot \eta(E) \mid \mathfrak{F}_{t_E}\right]$$

Where $\mathfrak{N} \subset \mathfrak{C}$ is the set of events which are not associated with any decision point, $\mathfrak{F}_t$ is the natural filtration at time t, and

$$\eta(E) = \begin{cases} 0, & \exists E_j \in \mathfrak{D}(E) \text{ such that } u_D = 0 \text{ for } E_j \in \Phi_D, \\ & \text{or } \exists E_i \in \mathfrak{X}(E) \text{ such that } u_D = 1 \text{ for } E_i \in \Phi_D \\ 1, & \text{otherwise} \end{cases}$$

represents whether or not an event E is realized based on its dependency on and exclusivity to other events. Note that $\eta(E)$ is $\mathfrak{F}_{t_E}$-measurable.

In practice the following three additional factors are applied:

1. A discount rate or term structure is applied to adjust for time value.

2. Each event can have an associated probability of occurrence or failure given that it is realized.

3. Value may be assigned to setting any given control decision to 0, representing a salvage or abandonment value.

4. The estimate efficiency functions are calibrated to reflect how quickly the user believes information with be gathered on the true value of the corresponded event.

Bibliography

Adner, Ron and Levinthal, Daniel. "Demand Heterogeneity and Technology Evolution: Implications for Product and Process Innovation." *Management Science* 47:5 (2001).

Alessandri, Todd M., Ford, David N., Lauder, Diane M., Leggio, Karyl B. and Taylor, Marilyn. "Managing Risk and Uncertainty in Complex Capital Projects." *Quarterly Review of Economics and Finance* 44:5 (2004) 751–767.

Baden-Fuller, Charles, Dean, Allison, McNamara, Peter and Hilliard, Bill. "Raising the Returns to Venture Finance." *Journal of Business Venturing*, August 2005.

Barringer, Bruce R., Jones, Foard F. and Neubaum, Donald O. "A Quantitative Content Analysis of the Characteristics of Rapid-Growth Firms and Their Founders." *Journal of Business Venturing* 20:5 (2005) 663–687.

Beer, Michael and Hohria, Nitin. "Cracking the Code of Change." *Harvard Business Review*, May-June 2000.

Benner, Mary J. and Tushman, Michael L. "Exploitation, Exploration, and Process Management: The Productivity Dilemma Revisited." *Academy of Management Review* 28:2, April 2003, 0363–7425.

Bhattacharya, Mousumi and Wright, Patrick M. "Managing Human Assets in an Uncertain World: Applying Real Options Theory to HRM." *International Journal of Human Resource Management* 16:6 (2005): 929–948.

Bowman, Edward H. and Moskowitz, Gary T. "Real Options Analysis and Strategic Decision Making." *Organization Science*, 12:6, November-December 2001, 772–777.

Chakravorti, Bhaskar. "The New Rules for Bringing Innovation to Market." *Harvard Business Review*, March 2004.

Chen, Jiyao, Reilly, Richard R., and Lynn, Gary S. "The Impacts of Speed-to-Market on New Product Success: The Moderating Effects of Uncertainty." *IEEE Transactions on Engineering Management* 52:2, May 2005.

Christensen, Clayton M., Anthony, Scott D. and Roth, Erik A. *Seeing What's Next* (Boston: Harvard Business School Press, 2004).

Clark, Matthew A., editor. *Mastering the Innovation Challenge Unleashing Growth and Creating Competitive Advantage*. Booz Allen Hamilton Inc. 2006.

Coy, Peter. "Exploiting Uncertainty: The 'Real-Options' Revolution in Decision-Making." *Business Week*, June 7, 1999.

Day, George S. and Schoemaker, Paul J. H. "Scanning the Periphery." *Harvard Business Review*, November 2005.

DiMasi, Joseph A., Hansen, Ronald W., and Grabowski, Henry G. "The Price of Innovation: New Estimates of Drug Development Costs." *Journal of Health Economics* 22 (2003) 151–185.

Fallon, Bernard V., Arcese, Anthony, and Hudson, Kisha. "Growth Restarts." Corporate Strategy Board (2003).

Fallows, James. "What do TiVo and the Mac Mini Have in Common?" *New York Times*, October 13, 2005.

Fichman, Robert G., Keil, Mark, and Tiwana, Amrit. "Beyond Valuation: Options Thinking in IT Project Management." *California Management Review* 47:2, Winter 2005.

Finkelstein, Sydney. *Why Smart Executives Fail*. New York: Penguin Group, 2003.

Ford, David N. and Sobek, Durward K. "Adapting Real Options to New Product Development by Modeling the Second Toyota Paradox." *IEEE Transactions on Engineering Management* 52:2, May 2005.

Foster, Richard and Kaplan, Sarah. *Creative Destruction* (New York: Currency Books, 2001).

Franklin, Carl. *Why Innovation Fails*. London: Spiro Press, 2003.

Ghoshal, Sumantra and Bartlett, Christopher A. "Changing the Role of Top Management: Beyond Structure to Processes." *Harvard Business Review*, January-February 1995.

Gilbert, Clark and Bower, Joseph L. "Disruptive Change: When Trying Harder Is Part of the Problem." *Harvard Business Review*, May 2002.

Gonzales, Laurence. *Deep Survival*. New York: W.W. Norton & Company, 2005.

Hindo, Brian. "At 3M, A Struggle Between Efficiency and Creativity." *Business Week*, June 11, 2007.

Kahneman, Daniel and Riepe, Mark W. "Aspects of Investor Psychology." *Journal of Portfolio Management* 24:4, Summer 1998.

Kenyon, Chris and Tompaidis, Stathis. "Real Options in Leasing: The Effect of Idle Time." *Operations Research* 49:5, September-October 2001, 675–689.

Kumar, M. V. Shyam. "The Value from Acquiring and Divesting a Joint Venture: A Real Options Approach." *Strategic Management Journal* 26 (2005) 321–331.

Kumar, Nirmalya. "Strategies to Fight Low Cost Rivals." *Harvard Business Review*, December 2006.

Laurie, Donald L., Doz, Yves L., and Sheer, Claude P. "Creating New Growth Platforms." *Harvard Business Review*, May, 2006.

Mackey, Jim and Välikangas, Liisa. "The Myth of Unbounded Growth." *MIT Sloan Management Review* 45:2, Winter 2004.

MacMillan, Ian C. and McGrath, Rita Gunther. "Discovering New Points of Differentiation." *Harvard Business Review*, July-August 1997.

Martin, Roger. "How Successful Leaders Think." *Harvard Business Review*, June, 2007.

McGrath, Rita G. and Boisot, Max. "Options Complexes: Going Beyond Real Options Reasoning." *E:CO* 7:2 (2005) 2–13.

McGrath, Rita Gunther. "Falling Forward: Real Options Reasoning and Entrepreneurial Failure." *Academy of Management Review* 24, January 1999.

Miller, Luke T. and Park, Chan S. "A Learning Real Options Framework with Application to Process Design and Capacity Planning." *Production and Operations Management*, Spring 2005, 5–20.

Nohria, Nitin, Joyce, William, and Roberson, Bruce. "What Really Works." *Harvard Business Review*, July 2003.

O'Connor, Gina Colarelli and Rice, Mark P. "Opportunity Recognition and Breakthrough Innovation in Large Established Firms." *California Management Review* 43:2, Winter 2001.

Pompe, Paul P. M. and Bilderbeek, Jan. "The Prediction of Bankruptcy of Small and Medium- Sized Industrial Firms." *Journal of Business Venturing* 20:6 (2005) 847–868.

Raynor, Michael E. *The Strategy Paradox*. New York: Currency Books, 2007.

Reurer, Jeffery J. and Tong, Tony W. "Real Options in International Joint Ventures." *Journal of Management* 3:3. June 2005, 403–423.

Sharma, Amol, Wingfield, Nick, and Yuan, Li. "How Steve Jobs Played Hardball in the iPhone Birth." *The Wall Street Journal*, January 17, 2007.

Silvert, Henry M. and Karpain, Greg. "Mid-Market CEO Challenge 2006." The Conference Board, 2006.

Smit, Han T. J. "Infrastructure Investment as a Real Options Game: The Case of European Airport Expansion." *Financial Management*, Winter 2003, 27–57.

Smith, James E. "Alternative Approaches for Solving Real-Options Problems." *Decision Analysis* 2:2, June 2005, 89–102.

Staw, Barry M. "The Escalation of Commitment to a Course of Action." *Academy of Management Review* 6:4 (1981) 577–587.

Staw, Barry M. and Epstein, Lisa D. "What Bandwagons Bring: Effects of Popular Management Techniques on Corporate Performance, Reputation, and CEO Pay." *Administrative Science Quarterly* 45:3, September 2000, 523.

Sutcliffe, Kathleen M. and Weber, Klaus. "The High Cost of Accurate Knowledge." *Harvard Business Review*, May 2003.

Tong, Tony W. and Reuer, Jeffrey J. "Firm and Industry Influences on the Value of Growth Options." *Strategic Organization* 4:1, 71–95.

Trigeorgis, Lenos. "Making Use of Real Options Simple: An Overview and Applications in Flexible / Modular Decision Making." *Engineering Economist* 50 (2005) 25–53.

Troy, Katherine. "Making Innovation Work, from Strategy to Practice." The Conference Board, 2006.

Zook, Chris. *Orchestrating Adjacency Moves: Strengthening the Core Versus Investing in Adjacencies* (Boston: Harvard Business School Press, 2006).

INDEX

Ⅲ Wharton School Publishing

In the face of accelerating turbulence and change, business leaders and policy makers need new ways of thinking to sustain performance and growth.

Wharton School Publishing offers a trusted source for stimulating ideas from thought leaders who provide new mental models to address changes in strategy, management, and finance. We seek out authors from diverse disciplines with a profound understanding of change and its implications. We offer books and tools that help executives respond to the challenge of change.

Every book and management tool we publish meets quality standards set by The Wharton School of the University of Pennsylvania. Each title is reviewed by the Wharton School Publishing Editorial Board before being given Wharton's seal of approval. This ensures that Wharton publications are timely, relevant, important, conceptually sound or empirically based, and implementable.

To fit our readers' learning preferences, Wharton publications are available in multiple formats, including books, audio, and electronic.

To find out more about our books and management tools, visit us at whartonsp.com and Wharton's executive education site, exceed.wharton.upenn.edu.

UNIVERSITY *of* PENNSYLVANIA